The

Public
Library

The
Public
Library

David McMenemy

facet publishing

© David McMenemy 2009

Published by
Facet Publishing
7 Ridgmount Street
London WC1E 7AE
www.facetpublishing.co.uk

Facet Publishing is wholly owned by
CILIP: the Chartered Institute of Library
and Information Professionals.

PEFC
PEFC/16-33-111
CATG-PEFC-052
www.pefc.org

Text printed on PEFC accredited material. The
policy of Facet Publishing is to use papers that
are natural, renewable and recyclable products,
made from wood grown in sustainable forests.
In the manufacturing process of our books,
and to further our policy, preference is given to
printers that have FSC and PEFC Chain of
Custody certification. The FSC and/or PEFC
logos will appear on those books where full
certification has been granted to the printer
concerned.

*British Library Cataloguing in Publication
Data*
A catalogue record for this book is
available from the British Library.

ISBN 978-1-85604-616-9

First published 2009

Typeset from author's disk in 11/15 pt
University Old Style and Nimbus Sans by
Facet Publishing.
Printed and made in Great Britain by
MPG Books Ltd, Bodmin, Cornwall.

For my parents
Mary Ferrier McIntyre McMenemy
and
Andrew McMenemy

Contents

Acknowledgements

My sincere thanks to the many people whose assistance I found invaluable in producing this book.

I'm very grateful to Facet Publishing for their excellent support and patience with me in writing the text, especially to Helen Carley, Louise Le Bas and Lin Franklin.

Thanks also to my colleagues in the Department of Computer and Information Sciences at the University of Strathclyde, and co-authors on *Librarianship: an introduction*, Gobinda Chowdhury, Paul Burton and Alan Poulter, for understanding the pressures of working to two simultaneous book deadlines! I am also grateful to my research student Christine Rooney-Browne for pointing out important reading and for sharing her inspiring views about social value, and to Briony Birdi of the University of Sheffield for her insightful chats about reader development.

Finally to the excellent public librarians I have worked for and with in the past, some retired, some moved on to pastures new, and some still fighting the good fight, I owe all of you a debt of gratitude. There are too many to mention but notable among those who deserve thanks are Stephen Finnie, Alex Tomeny, Margaret Houston, Carmela Vezza, David Boyd, Harry Stewart, Murdoch Nicholson, Dan McCallum, Gerry Torley, Jim Black, Biff Carmichael, John McGuire, John Burke and Hamish Whyte.

Each of you contributed in some way to this text, with your passion for public libraries, and your professionalism.

Thank you all.

David McMenemy

Preface

Aims

The goal of this book is to provide an introductory text on the development of public libraries in the UK and the range of services provided by them in the 21st century. Discussions will focus on the history of the public library and its development into the modern era, and the book will describe the nature of services commonly provided by modern public libraries, and how those services are governed and administered.

Public libraries mean many things to many people. They are at once independent, but political. They lend resources of high cultural value as well as material many commentators believe to be of poor quality and not suitable for funding from the public purse. Yet they have stood for generations as instruments of the higher values of society, and remain among our most prized public institutions. They represent the ideal that everyone within society deserves the right to access materials for their educational, cultural and leisure benefit, regardless of their income level, political beliefs, race, creed or colour.

It is fair to say that if the public library concept had not yet been invented, anyone proposing such a simple but worthy idea would be lauded as someone of great vision and charity. Undoubtedly every community served by a public library across the globe is better for that institution, both its staff and contents, being a part of it. Yet although most people would acknowledge that public libraries are a positive influence for their community and society, these libraries continually find themselves battling to justify their existence and their right to access the essential public funds they require to exist and grow.

The author unashamedly takes that stance that public libraries are institutions that we must cherish, although we must seek to understand and value the services provided by them in their entirety before we can truly do so. In a world where public finances are under pressure to ensure that civically funded services are achieving the best possible value for money for citizens, regrettably public libraries have to justify every penny. However, in doing so they should not compromise their mission for short-term or political motives.

Book structure: public library service strands

For simplicity, the book will be organized into three distinct sections:

1 The public library: history and modern context
2 Service themes of the modern public library
3 Issues in management and service development

The approach is to recognize the distinctive history of public libraries, why they came about, what services they now offer, and what challenges are presented in the modern era for the librarian delivering them.

After an introduction to the modern context of public libraries, Part 1 will continue with a history of public libraries, from their early origins through to their development as the modern services we know today.

Part 2 will discuss in detail the nature of services provided by the modern public library. To facilitate easier discussion, this section will be divided into four chapters focused on specific service themes:

1 *Equity of access*: these are services provided to ensure a library service is socially inclusive and reaches all its community equally. In addition to the traditional services that will be discussed, specific examples can consist of services for housebound users, disabled users, or users from ethnic minority backgrounds. It could be argued that equity of access is the key mission for public libraries, since it is about including all.

2 *Cultural and leisure roles*: under this category we will discuss the traditional roles of lending books and other media, such as DVDs, videos, music formats and video games. Within this broader framework we will also discuss the nature of book lending and reading promotion, reader development and the promotion of the public library as a cultural focus for its community.

3 *Information, advice and informed citizenship*: this is another traditional public library role, which covers non-fiction materials, reference enquiries, community information, web and intranet provision, and heritage and digitization services. In addition many public library services are incorporating partnerships with other public services and offering one-stop shops for advice. This can consist of health advice, social security and benefits advice, and perhaps also careers advice. Citizenship also relates to the role of the public library in ensuring citizens have a route to engage with their elected representatives. Services include access to pan-national, national and local e-government via community portals.

4 *Lifelong learning*: this is a core service strand, which in the modern context involves issues such as reader development, ICT skills, literacy and numeracy.

This is a broad range of service strands, and it is clear that although their main service is lending books, modern public libraries have roles in other areas that equally need to be understood in terms of their importance, and also measured appropriately for effectiveness. For a complete picture of impact and effectiveness to be determined, one must consider the totality of services that public libraries provide in the modern era.

The strands under discussion are all inter-related in that, for example, lifelong learning can be fostered by online resources, by print and media materials, by community groups running events in the library, and by linking with schools and other appropriate agencies, both local and national. There will be an inevitable degree of overlap within the discussion of each strand; however, this should serve to highlight how some services satisfy multiple community needs, for example reading for leisure and reading for lifelong learning. Equally, however, such overlaps can also illustrate the tensions between those roles some commentators see as appropriate to the public library and others they feel the library should not be undertaking. This particular debate is one that is not new, as we will see.

The third section of the book will examine management and service development issues in public libraries. Chapters will focus on the management challenges such as budgeting within local authority frameworks, ethical issues and the sustainability of digital services. This section will also discuss performance measurement of public libraries. Finally there will be a spotlight on marketing and branding, and how this is leading to a reconsideration of infrastructure issues, such as buildings and design. In this section we will also discuss the various rebranding initiatives that have sought to reinvent the concept of the public library for a modern audience.

It is hoped that the book will give an accurate picture of the services provided by modern public libraries and how they are governed, financed and managed. It is also hoped that the reader gets a comprehensive picture of the issues related to professional practice in public libraries, the groups and organizations that support working in the sector, and the issues of professional concern that currently predominate.

The perceived audience for the book is wide; but should librarians from within and without the public library sector and students of LIS feel that the book has painted a broad and realistic picture of modern public libraries, then the author will feel that the book has achieved its purpose.

David McMenemy

Part 1

The public library: history and modern context

Chapter 1

Public libraries: the modern context

Introduction

As an evolving collection of national institutions, public libraries have been in existence for over 150 years, and for much longer as a series of ad hoc libraries serving local communities. Over that period they have grown from being an informal network to a nationwide, statutorily accountable service.

In recent years there have been several key reports that have examined the UK public library sector and its perceived challenges. These have come from varying sources including the expected government advisory departments as well as advocacy groups and think tanks. A key strand in all of them is the desire to create a modern mission for the public library within the information society. How for instance does an idea that was adopted in the Victorian era to enhance access to learning and knowledge remain relevant in an age when many people now have such access within their homes via the world wide web? All of this has led to what has been dubbed as a volatile time for its history (Goulding, 2006, 3).

To set the scene for the remainder of the book, this chapter will discuss some of the recent discourse around public libraries in the UK, with emphasis on key government reports and contributions to the discussion from researchers in public librarianship, and interested other parties such as library advocacy groups.

The 21st century context

The picture of the public library service in the UK in any given period can be accurately gleaned from the twin publications of the Library and Information Statistics Unit (LISU) entitled *Annual Library Statistics* and *Public Libraries Material Fund and Budget Survey*. According to *Annual Library Statistics*, during 2004-5:

■ Public library expenditure increased for the seventh consecutive year, to £18.32 per head of population.

■ Although the greatest part of this was on library staff, over £95 million was spent on books with a further £29 million on audiovisual and electronic materials. Increasing staff costs reflect in part an increase in opening hours.

■ The number of visits to public libraries continued to increase, although fewer books are being borrowed overall. An estimated 48% of the adult population visit the library each year, drawn in part by the information and communications technology (ICT) facilities available in 97% of branches.

■ The proportion of children's books in stock has been increasing, and issues of children's material had increased for the first time since 1996-7.   (LISU, 2006)

Thus libraries remain popular public institutions in the UK, with large swathes of the population in active membership and regularly using their services. The statistics also reflect an evolving service, with the introduction of information and communications technology (ICT) facilities via the People's Network programme offering a new service strand for many library authorities and one that is proving popular across the country.

Yet as the service evolves it also seeks to deliver traditional services alongside the new, and this brings potential tensions. ICT facilities require space in the library building for equipment, and with the introduction of the People's Network this space often had to be provided at the expense of space previously devoted to book shelving or other support for the traditional services.

Thus the traditional has had to learn to co-exist with the modern, and this has been a fundamental theme for the public library sector in the 21st century, in terms of service ethos, infrastructure and staff roles.

Public libraries and modern life

As will be seen in Chapter 2, one of the key motivations for those who first advocated the introduction of public libraries in the mid 19th century was for the working classes to use their leisure time in culturally beneficial ways. Certainly in this period several major factors influenced how people spent their leisure time: mainly lack of money, and a lack of interesting leisure options to keep them entertained and amused. In the 21st century this is no longer an issue for the majority of the population as standards of living rise and they have more disposable income to spend on their leisure pursuits. People also have more leisure options, such as restaurants, theatre, cinema, television, DVDs, travel, book clubs and many more. This essentially means that public libraries may no longer be fulfilling as much of a leisure role for people as they used to, even recently.

There are two ways of addressing such a scenario. One is to attempt to position the public library as a viable leisure option in competition with others that exist and thus aggressively market it to its local community in a modern way to be seen as a potential cultural and leisure option for all. The alternative is to accept that as a public service the library simply cannot or should not compete in this way with other commercial options and instead should target its potential users in a more strategic way, aiming services more directly at users with special needs and those who are excluded from society. Although public libraries are charged with offering services for the entire community, realistically many within the community do not wish to use the services or simply do not need to. In such an environment marketing and selection of the user groups to market to becomes an immensely important decision.

The issue of targeting will be touched on in the discussion of government reports below, and in more detail in Chapter 3.

Politics and public libraries

The relationship of the library profession with the Conservative Government that was in power in the UK from 1979 to 1997 could be most accurately described as tetchy. It was broadly felt within the profession that the Conservative ideals prevalent in the 1980s and the subsequent cuts to local government were incompatible with a high quality public library service. There was also a feeling that the then government was keen on privatizing or charging for public services where possible, and the publication in 1986 of *Ex Libris*, a report advocating this by the Conservative think tank the Adam Smith Institute, did not help the relationship between profession and government (Adam Smith Institute, 1986).

The election of the New Labour Government in 1997 was generally felt to be an opportunity for public libraries to be placed back on the political agenda. The party had been keen to position combating social exclusion at the heart of its political mission, and identified early on the role of the public library in aiding this mission. This was a commonsense approach, since the national network of public libraries across the country was well placed at the heart of many communities that the government had identified as being socially excluded. The potential politicization of the profession notwithstanding, public librarians could see a more clearly defined role for their services through the political priorities of the new government.

However it would be churlish to suggest that the Conservative policies that rankled with the profession for so long were completely forgotten with the introduction of the New Labour administration. The emphasis on quantitative performance measurement, more commercialism in the public sector, and the quest to modernize and transform public services was as much a policy backbone of New Labour as it was the previous administration.

Government publications

The Museums Libraries and Archives Council (MLA) is the advisory body for libraries in England. It operates as a non-departmental public body responsible to the Department for Culture, Media and Sport (DCMS), its role to lead strategically on public library development in England, and its reports have a major influence on the development of public libraries. Discussion of some of the more service-specific reports will take place in

Chapters 3 to 6 where appropriate, but, for the purposes of this context-setting chapter, three documents will be highlighted in more detail: *Framework for the Future* (DCMS, 2003), *Blueprint for Excellence* (Dolan, 2007) and a DCMS Select Committee Report published in 2005.

Framework for the Future

The Department for Culture, Media and Sport published its major vision for public libraries in 2003. *Framework for the Future* sought to establish a set of principles for the service to build a new vision around. The vision was to encompass four key strands:

- *evolution*: building on libraries' traditional core skills in promoting reading, informal learning and self-help
- *public value*: focusing on areas where public intervention will deliver the largest benefits to society including support for adult literacy and pre-school learning
- *distinctiveness*: building on libraries' open, neutral and self-help culture; they should not duplicate the efforts of other public and private sector providers but complement them through partnership working
- *local interpretations of national programmes*: developing national programmes that will raise the profile of the public library service as a whole but which are sufficiently flexible to be adapted to local needs.

(DCMS, 2003)

And these in turn should be built around three service strands:

- the promotion of reading and informal learning
- access to digital skills and services including e-government
- implementing measures to tackle social exclusion, build community identity and develop citizenship.

(DCMS, 2003)

It was no surprise that the service strands mirrored New Labour's own government priorities, which included lifelong learning, expansion of the digital economy, and targeting of social exclusion. Thus it could be seen that the document placed the public library as a key facilitator in delivering central government priorities.

At the root of the report was the need for public libraries to engage more with their communities and assert their roles in partnership with other local government organizations and groups within the community. The report featured various case studies to highlight best practice on each of the visionary strands, notably highlighting success stories where communities had seen their library rebuilt into a modern, vibrant community space. Other case studies highlighted libraries that had experimented with innovative service provision, such as enhanced opening hours and rebranding initiatives.

The report also advocated more of a role in such partnerships for the private sector, highlighting the successes achieved by The Reading Agency in attracting sponsorship for national reading programmes, as well as successes in Private Finance Initiative contracts between local authorities and private companies to finance the construction of new library buildings.

The key researcher involved in the project was Charles Leadbetter who worked for the think tank Demos. He revisited his work in a later publication commissioned by a library advocacy group, as will be seen below.

Blueprint for Excellence

In early 2007 the MLA produced a consultation document that sought to test a vision for the public library service for the period 2008-11 (Dolan, 2007). The vision was encapsulated under six propositions for public libraries. The first three proposals are focused around the purpose and role of libraries in the modern era and the challenges inherent in delivering them:

- Proposition 1 - the purpose of the public library - is to be:
    - focused on reading, knowledge of all kinds and formats, essential information, and the active engagement of the library in community cohesion and life
- Proposition 2 - the key roles of the public library - are to be a:
    - community place, where communities can engage with knowledge in a safe and comfortable environment

  - development agency, where the library partners other groups to enhance community skills
  - digital library, providing access to digital content and the equipment to access it
- Proposition 3 – nine key challenges for improvement – are to provide:
  - a clear definition of what library users can expect from their service as a national entitlement
  - funding: adequate resources to provide this level of service
  - partnership, and to work with partners of all sectors to deliver it
  - improved buildings and access: good opening hours and high quality facilities
  - what users want: comprehensive high quality stock
  - the digital library: access to library materials, 24/7 where possible
  - staff who are customer-focused and strategic
  - innovation, exploring new service models and partnerships
  - advocacy and research to raise awareness of quality service and celebrate success.   (Dolan, 2007, 6–7)

Dolan focuses on what he sees as fundamental questions for the future of the public library service, namely what the public should expect of them: 'it is time for the public library service to take a hard look at both its role in society and the services it can and should be providing' (Dolan, 2007, 6–7).

The other three propositions focus on what the final product the user will experience should look like, and how success can be measured. They are:

- Proposition 4 – essential elements for success
- Proposition 5 – what excellence will look like for people, communities and funders
- Proposition 6 – actions and outcomes 2008–11.

Blueprint for Excellence revisits some of the territory of previous reports, emphasizing user wants as the centre of the public library service, and reinforcing that the public library must be seen as a viable service that contributes to the community cohesion of everyone. It also emphasizes the importance of partnership working within both the public and the private sectors. Thus it mirrors policy areas discussed previously in *Framework for the Future*, suggesting the ongoing importance of these to the policy of the Labour Government.

DCMS Select Committee Report

In October 2004 the Culture, Media and Sport Select Committee of the House of Commons issued a call for evidence in its investigation of the state of UK public libraries. Specifically it was keen to investigate issues related to:

- accessibility
- funding
- new models of provision and new policy demands
- the legislative, strategic and administrative framework
- recruitment and training of library staff
- the role of institutional and specialist libraries
- performance and maintenance of the People's Network.

(Culture Media and Sport Committee, 2005)

The Committee gathered evidence and testimony in late 2004 and delivered its report to Parliament in February 2005.

The subsequent report is perhaps the most holistic look at public libraries in the modern era, since evidence was gathered from stakeholders of all backgrounds, professional, governmental, advocacy and public. The Committee addressed several key issues related to services, funding and staffing. For instance it advocated that public libraries should re-emphasize their core mission: 'We are in no doubt that, while libraries are about more than books (and newspapers and journals), these traditional materials must be the bedrock upon which the library services rest no matter how the institution is refreshed or re-branded in the light of local consultation' (Culture Media and Sport Committee, 2005, 44).

The Committee had concerns that there was a danger of placing too much pressure on libraries in terms of delivering community enhancement agendas outwith their core mission: 'Libraries and their staff cannot be expected to constitute a one-stop shop for all a community's demands for information and advice without the appropriate allocation, and clear demarcation, of resources' (44).

The Committee encouraged library authorities to allocate more money to the provision of books, suggesting that '[a] substantial increase in the percentage of funding spent by each library authority on books should be a priority' (45). Concerns were raised regarding the public library infrastructure, and, while acknowledging some excellent examples of newbuilds, the report suggested that putting right the crumbling infrastructure would cost £240–650 million.

Other issues highlighted by the report included the need for public library staff to be recruited from a wider pool of talents, including staff with skills in: 'knowledge management; IT; leadership; public relations and customer service expertise; managers; business-minded people; those qualified in marketing and finance; web management and many more' (39).

There was also a need to focus on leadership issues within the profession and to 'recognise its shortcomings in this area of leadership and advocacy and plan both to train its staff internally and to recruit people with appropriate experience from outside the profession' (39).

The Coates Report

Public libraries also see great interest in their role from those outside government. As publicly funded institutions that spend a great deal of public money each year, it is inevitable that advocacy groups are very interested in exactly how that money is spent.

Perhaps the most controversial report to be produced in recent times was published by the Libri Trust in partnership with the LASER Foundation. The Libri Trust was a charity that aimed to 'encourage a vibrant and relevant public library network, focused on its prime responsibility of providing the public with a good choice of books for reading and reference' (Libri Trust, 2005). It had a belief in what public libraries should be and felt that the service they provided had declined:

> We believe that the public library service has important lessons to learn from all sectors of the book trade and the information provision sector. Learning the lessons will help create a public library service that is efficient, serves the needs of local communities and maintains public libraries as the heart of community life.
>
> (Libri Trust, 2005)

The LASER (London and South Eastern Library Region) Foundation had operated for over 70 years as a regional interest group for libraries in that part of England. It became a grant-making trust in 2001 and dispersed the remainder of its funds in commissioning research into public libraries in the UK. *Who's in Charge* (Coates, 2004), commonly referred to as the Coates Report after its author Tim Coates, was perhaps the most widely known report of its kind commissioned under the auspices of the LASER Foundation.

The main thesis of the Coates Report was that libraries were in decline and risked becoming obsolete in a period of 10–15 years if current usage figures continued to develop at their current rate. The reason for this decline was obvious to Coates (7):

> because their local libraries have poor selections of books and reading material, they have short opening hours and they are often inconveniently situated, dilapidated and, even, unsafe to work in. The public does not want a new kind of library; they just want a good efficient library that is up to date and pleasant to use.

Coates was also critical of what he saw as a dangerous emphasis for reports into libraries to be aimed at the profession, when in reality only councillors and perhaps senior officials had the power to make any significant changes to the state of libraries. The main recommendations of the report called on councillors in local authorities to:

- treble expenditure on books and reading material
- increase opening hours by 50%
- institute a programme of library redecoration and redesign.

Crucially Coates believed that all of the above should be done within existing resources through the introduction of efficiencies. Criticism of the report from within the profession was prevalent, with some questioning how such improvements could be made with no additional funding. The report was also criticized for using one authority, Hampshire County Library Service, as the basis for the research. Coates has subsequently developed a Good Library Blog (www.goodlibraryguide.com/blog/) to continue his campaign for the improvement of public libraries.

The LASER Foundation also funded follow-on work on *Framework for the Future* from the consultant who authored that report (Leadbetter, 2003). The report, entitled *Overdue*, cited the case of Singapore's national public library system, and one of Leadbetter's key proposals was the formation of a National Libraries Development Agency (NLDA) in England to allow co-ordination of policy and practice. A key argument of the report was that it was difficult to create a national network of quality when the funding for that network is agreed and administered locally. Thus local authority priorities can mean libraries have funding cut in one authority and increased in others, leading to an imbalance in provision. Leadbetter's warning was stark, however, suggesting that: 'Libraries are sleepwalking to disaster, it's time they woke up' (Leadbetter, 2003, 35).

Research on public libraries

Although government bodies and advocacy groups fund specific aspects of public library research, within the university departments that continue to teach librarianship as a degree subject the efficacy of research into public library topics remains strong, especially at two of the foremost schools in the subject, the University of Sheffield and Loughborough University. In both institutions some excellent work continues to be done into the major issues facing public libraries, and at all departments in the UK teaching librarianship a continuing stream of Masters students annually investigate the challenges through their dissertation research.

Perhaps most notably the Centre for the Public Library and Information in Society (CPLIS) based in the University of Sheffield's Department of Information Studies has undertaken major research into public library impact, performance measurement and reader development. Thus issues around public libraries and their users continue to be important areas not only of professional and political concern, but also of academic concern.

Service challenges

Although any public service always faces challenges, the nature of what public libraries exist to do means they face challenges that are unique to them as well as challenges that are general and impact on the entire public sector.

Falling price of books

Members of the public can purchase copies of books more easily now than ever before. The most notable reason for this is the collapse of the Net Book Agreement (NBA) and the subsequent growth in book selling cheaply through the internet and supermarkets.

The NBA coloured book selling for almost the entire 20th century. This was an agreement between publishers and booksellers that books on sale would only be sold for the price agreed by the publishers themselves. Any bookseller deviating from this stance risked having all supplies from that publisher ended. The NBA was obviously useful for both publisher and bookseller, since it kept the price of books relatively high, which benefited both parties. The NBA also benefited libraries from a service standpoint, since the high cost of hardback books in particular meant that borrowing from the library was an alternative that was attractive to many avid readers.

The NBA began to unravel in the mid 1990s when some larger booksellers began to offer discounts. This was followed by the examination of the agreement by the Office of Fair Trading, and it was clear that the 90-odd-year history of the agreement from this point onwards was coming to an end. Several large publishers withdrew from the agreement in 1995, and it was finally deemed illegal in 1997.

The collapse of the agreement led to many more outlets for book buying for the public. Supermarkets began to use their buying power to sell on books with heavy discounts, and large booksellers also sold books at a great discount. There is no question that this led to people who may have been frequent library users in the past being more able to purchase books, and the effect of the collapse of the NBA on the usage of libraries cannot be underestimated.

Retail model

Bookshops responded positively in the 1990s to customer lifestyle expectations by focusing on making their premises more user friendly. The modern bookshop is now a lifestyle facility where people can visit and read a book over a coffee before they decide to buy it. This fitted well into the 1990s coffee-house culture and has only gained in popularity as bookshops have increasingly become social as well as commercial spaces.

This has led to increasing calls for public libraries to mirror this development and learn from the benefits of the modern bookshop model. These developments and the advice given to public libraries on how to achieve them will be discussed more fully in Chapter 11.

New technologies

Public libraries serve a vital function in making ICTs available to the public. Although many homes now have fast and reliable access to the internet, a large portion of society remains disenfranchised from the information superhighway. Public libraries are in an excellent position to bridge this gap and help to close the digital divide. The provision of high quality ICTs via the People's Network programme created a culture of quality in provision of computer-based services, and despite the burden being passed on to local authorities once the sponsorship money ran out, regularly renewing these technologies is a key priority for public libraries.

Of course public libraries can do much more than just provide access; they can offer assistance in gaining competence with the technologies to enhance their lifelong learning role. Chapter 6 will discuss some of the initiatives currently in use to address this issue.

Equity and excellence

Recently a noted academic in the field of public librarianship in the UK, Bob Usherwood, has challenged what he feels is a culture of dumbing down by public libraries (Usherwood, 2007). The heart of his thesis is that public libraries are not being equitable in pandering to populist tastes at the expense of breadth of collection. In other words providing a professional public service is not always related to giving the public what they want; rather, the needs of the community require some consideration. He argues that 'Good professionals prescribe for a particular set of conditions, they do not always give people what they want' (2007, 26). Usherwood (2007, 4) is concerned that public libraries are increasingly seen as places of entertainment:

> Where a public library might once have been regarded as a place for study and reflection it is now primarily seen by some as a place of entertainment. Those in the profession who dare to argue against the current orthodoxy are attacked as traditionalists, and accused of ignoring social exclusion.

Usherwood also voices concern over the potential of the populist approach to lead to ignorance in the populace.

The emergence of the citizen-consumer

Linking to the themes discussed by Usherwood is the emergence of what has been dubbed the citizen-consumer. This is the notion that the public now interact with and expect the same levels of service from their public services as they do from any commercial service they deal with. The key issue is one of choice, that is the public have a choice in whether or not to use public libraries and public librarians need to ensure that the choice is an attractive one.

The notion of the citizen-consumer has had a great deal of political and professional capital in the UK, with discourse continually advocating a more commercial approach to service design and delivery. As previously mentioned, *Framework for the Future* advocated a larger role for the private sector in public library partnerships, and this was not merely related to issues of sponsorship but also to staff development in public libraries. For instance it is argued that librarians can learn better marketing and promotion skills by working with the private sector.

Expanding Usherwood's equity and excellence debate a little, it is yet to be proven how the choice paradigm can enhance equity. The belief that the citizen has a choice in whether to use the public library or not assumes that a viable alternative to the service exists elsewhere; although this may be true of paid services such as DVD or CD rental, it is difficult to see the efficacy of the argument in terms of free book lending. While bookshops may sell what public libraries lend, it makes comparisons superficial in nature.

Conclusion

Although the early years of the 21st century are undoubtedly an exciting period for the development of public libraries, there are also potential pitfalls for them in terms of the prevailing discourse. The over-arching emphasis of numerous studies initiated by the government and think tanks has been a call for a reappraisal of the public library model from the point of view of the needs of the internet age. Much of the language of the New Labour Government since 1997 has been about the transformation of public services, and public libraries have not been immune from such calls to modernize and change their ethos and outlook to be more responsive to the user needs of the modern population, and to prove their worth in this context through enhanced and expanded performance measurement criteria.

A common thread in all of the reports discussed is a quest to delineate a modern mission for the public library. In essence this is a desire to make the service relevant to the needs of the modern citizen, and ensure that it is done in as efficient a way as possible. This modern mission needs to encompass traditional and new services, and in practice often involves a re-imagining of environment and location for many public library authorities who feel that the old way of doing things no longer sustains enough interest with the public.

The politics of how public services are encouraged to see their users also has a major bearing on how services are professionally interpreted and delivered. The emergence through the politics of New Labour of the citizen-consumer has led to calls for public libraries to be more retail-like, and as will be seen in future chapters many are indeed becoming so. All of these factors have made for a challenging period for public library services in interpreting user needs and developing services that are relevant to them in the modern era.

The next chapter of the book will take a dip into the history and development of public libraries in the UK and explain how the modern network of service points we are now familiar with originated, and the social and political pressures that led to their ongoing evolution.

References

Adam Smith Institute (1986) *Ex Libris*, ASI (Research) Ltd.

Coates, T. (2004) *Who's in Charge? Responsibility for the public library service*, Libri Trust.

Culture, Media and Sport Committee (2005) *Public Libraries: third report of session 2004-5*, House of Commons, Culture, Media and Sport Committee.

DCMS (2003) *Framework for the Future: libraries, learning and information in the next decade*, Department for Culture, Media and Sport.

Dolan, J. (2007) *Blueprint for Excellence - public libraries 2008-2011: 'Connecting people to knowledge and inspiration'*, Museums, Libraries and Archives Council.

Goulding, A. (2006) *Public Libraries in the 21st Century: defining services and debating the future*, Ashgate.

Leadbetter, C. (2003) *Overdue: how to create a modern public library service*, Demos,
      www.demos.co.uk/files/overdue.pdf.

Libri Trust (2005) *Libri Trust: about us*,
      www.rwevans.co.uk/libri/about.htm.

LISU (2006) *Annual Library Statistics 2006*, Library and Information Statistics Unit,
      www.lboro.ac.uk/departments/ls/lisu/downloads/als06.pdf.

Usherwood, B. (2007) *Equity and Excellence in the Public Library: why ignorance is not our heritage*, Ashgate.

White, S. (2007) *Public Libraries Material Fund and Budget Survey 2006-2008*, Library and Information Statistics Unit,
      www.nielsenbookdata.co.uk/uploads/plmf-07_Final2.pdf.

Chapter 2

Historical development of public libraries in the UK

Introduction

Public libraries have existed for a comparatively short space of time in terms of human history. In the 21st century it is difficult to conceive of any large community in the developed world that does not have at least one public library, yet this was the case for the majority of the citizens of Victorian Britain. The network that currently exists in the UK owes its existence to a number of individuals who led the way either by altruistic provision of a library for their local community, or through their campaigning for a national network through parliament. As Black suggests, 'Proposals for a truly free library service did not appear overnight: they emerged on the back of a healthy tradition of independent library provision made by a diverse range of social, political and educational institutions' (Black, 1996, 26).

This chapter will discuss the antecedents of public libraries, the history of the public library movement in the UK, the progression towards the 1850 Act, and how the resultant system of public libraries developed into the 20th century.

The early antecedents

The origin of public libraries, using this term to describe libraries freely open to members of the public to consult the materials within, can be traced back long before the 1850 Act of Parliament that established the principle in law. The publishing revolution brought about by Johannes Gutenberg and his development of movable type took the production of books into a new era. Although books were still relatively expensive items well into the 19th century, the ability to mass produce texts meant that they were more readily available for purchase by benefactors or groups who wished to create libraries for their local communities. As Kelly has discussed, the term public library had been used widely from the 17th century to refer to libraries open to the public that had been endowed by such benefactors (Kelly, 1977, 4).

The first public library, as in a library freely accessible to the general public without restrictions, is commonly attributed to the library set up in the Free Grammar School in Coventry in 1601, which existed until 1913-14 (Minto, 1932, 22). Subsequent libraries were created in Norwich (1608), Bristol (1615), Leicester (1632) and Manchester – the famous Chetham Library in 1653 (Murison, 1971, 19). No one model accounts for all of these early libraries, as they were a mixture of endowed, subscription and parochial libraries. Although the discussion below will focus on each type in its own right, it must be noted that some of the antecedents were actually a combination of library types. For instance it was not uncommon for an endowed library also to be a parochial library as a result of the materials purchased for it or bequeathed to it by the benefactor. Kelly summarizes this potential confusion well:

> We thus have three main types of non-publicly maintained libraries: institutional libraries, endowed libraries, and subscription libraries. These three methods may be combined in various ways, e.g. a library may be created by endowment and maintained by subscription, or created by an institution and maintained by endowment, and so forth, but these three main principles are worth keeping in mind.
>
> (Kelly, 1966, 7)

Endowed libraries

An endowed library was a library that existed due to the generosity of an individual or individuals. This often occurred as a bequest on the death of the sponsor; however, it could also be an endowment in their lifetime.

The previously mentioned Chetham Library in Manchester is perhaps one of the most well known examples of an endowed library. Humphrey Chetham, the benefactor, was a Lancashire wool-factor and money-lender who bequeathed £1000 to set up a library in his name for the use of the local community. By 1826 the library had in excess of 14,000 volumes available for consultation.

Another example of an endowed library is Stirling's Library in Glasgow, formed in 1791 from a bequest by Walter Stirling, a city merchant. This library existed in various locations near its original site until 2002 when it moved into the basement of the Gallery of Modern Art and formed the basis of the library there. Another endowed library in Glasgow is the Mitchell Library, created at the bequest of Stephen Mitchell, a local tobacco baron. He left the sum of £70,000 to build and stock a library for the people of Glasgow.

Parish and other ecclesiastical libraries

Access to written knowledge in the middle ages and beyond was problematic for most citizens. The only realistic model for access was among the various institutions of the church, and as Kelly states almost every conceivable kind of ecclesiastical community had a collection of books for its clergy and other learned community members to discuss (Kelly, 1966, 9). These early libraries, housed in monasteries, churches and universities, were immensely protective of the valuable materials within, and this was not merely in terms of cultural value. Books before the invention of the printing press were extraordinarily valuable commodities as production by hand was a task that was extremely time consuming. The old image of libraries with books chained to large lecterns is a negative but accurate one, and many books were kept under strict lock and key by institutions desperate to ensure they would not lose their precious collections. Such libraries were hugely influential in the intellectual development of Europe, and also the development of cataloguing standards.

Parish libraries were a natural smaller extension of the ecclesiastical libraries that had been built up over the middle ages. Created primarily for ecclesiastical purposes by local clergymen or benefactors, their main purpose in most cases was for the continuing education of the clergy. This was an essential component of the clergyman's role in his community, the ability to dispense knowledge and wisdom. However, to say there was one model for parochial libraries would be incorrect. While many contained only religious texts, others contained works on other topics such as history. That said, the growth in literacy meant that even libraries that were predominantly based around theological collections still offered readers the chance to build on their literacy skills and spread a reading culture within communities: 'Though the books in such libraries seem to us dauntingly theological, it would be wrong to assume that they were never read' (Kelly, 1966, 18).

Subscription libraries

Subscription libraries offered access to members for a fee, normally an annual payment. Kelly (1966, 26) offers three models of subscription libraries that were popular:

- private subscription libraries
- book clubs
- circulating libraries.

Britain's industrial growth also led to a desire for knowledge among those classes who were prospering from the industrial revolution and the wealth it was creating. The industrial centres especially saw a rise in the number of groups that were formed around intellectual discourse, evidenced by the formation of groups like the Manchester Literary and Philosophical Society in 1781 (Kelly and Kelly, 1977, 47). Such groups offered the opportunity to pool resources and create a collection of materials for members to borrow.

   The earliest examples of what were dubbed gentlemen's subscription libraries were found in Scotland in the mid 18th century, with libraries at Dumfries, Kelso and Ayr of prominence (Kelly and Kelly, 1977, 50). The London Library remains one of the finest examples of a working subscription library. Formed in 1841, it numbered some of the greatest literary figures of the Victorian era as members, Thomas Carlyle, William

Thackeray, George Eliot and Charles Dickens all being members in the early days of the library. To this day luminaries from all aspects of the literary world are members.

Mechanics' institutes

Another important development in shaping the notion of public libraries was the spread of mechanics' institute libraries. Mechanics' institutes were formed in local communities for mechanics, engineers and other working people to offer a means of sharing texts on professional subjects, as well as offering lectures and courses on matters of interest. The roots of the movement can be traced back to the work of Professor George Birkbeck of the Andersonian Institute (now the University of Strathclyde) who began in 1800 to provide lectures on the 'mechanical arts' for the local mechanics in Glasgow, which inevitably led to a library being formed to support the subjects under study. These lectures subsequently led to the formation of the first mechanics' institute in 1821 in Glasgow and the movement spread nationwide, with 400 such bodies in the UK by 1849 and over 700 by 1863 (McColvin, 1956, 22).

An account of the services on offer in the Glasgow Mechanics' Institute is given by Hendry where he tells us that the 'institution was founded by the mechanics of Glasgow, for obtaining instruction in the useful branches of knowledge, especially those connected with the arts, and was opened to all classes of the community' (Hendry, 1974, 21). Membership of the institute was available for a fee of 4 shillings, which allowed attendance at lectures and courses in topics such as chemistry and mechanics. Membership also allowed borrowing rights to a collection of over 6700 volumes (Hendry, 1974, 21).

As well as forming the basis for many of the public libraries formed in the late Victorian era some modern universities in the UK were also influenced by mechanics' institutes. These include Heriot-Watt University, University of Manchester Institute of Science and Technology (UMIST), the University of Strathclyde and Birkbeck College, now part of the University of London and named in honour of George Birkbeck who continued his adult education work after moving to London. Their emphasis on providing access to books for their members played a crucial part in the raising of the educational attainment of the working classes, and led inevitably to the demand from some quarters for a more robust system of rate supported libraries for local communities. The role of mechanics' institutes in creating a culture of learning among many in the working classes was a major catalyst in the development of publicly supported libraries in the UK.

Other antecedents

In the early part of the 19th century an ambitious plan was formulated by the Reverend Samuel Brown, a Minister in the Scottish county of East Lothian. His plan was to formulate a series of 'itinerating libraries' whereby 50 books would be placed in each village of a county, and after a period of two years this stock would be circulated to other villages, and would continue to move round every two years to be replaced by a collection from another village. He began his plan in 1817, and by 1835 there were over 2000 volumes circulating around 47 libraries (Kent et al., 1978, 269). Although the purpose behind such a project was to provide appropriate textbooks on religious subjects, the libraries also contained material of a 'plain and popular nature' on a variety of topics in the arts and sciences (Kent et al., 1978, 269).

The public library movement

Public libraries can still be seen as social education vehicles for their communities; although they were not designed to offer formal education akin to schools or colleges, they have always formed a self-improvement function for many of their users, and can be seen in light of the great social improvement movement that was a popular cause of the Victorian middle classes.

The desire to create a more formal system of public libraries was driven by several factors, ranging from social to economic. The Industrial Revolution had transformed British society from being largely agrarian, to one based around vast urban centres, where working-class communities sprung up to support the major evolving industries, such as mining and cotton spinning. This necessary evil for economic development brought with it large numbers of people with little to do outside their working hours, and concern grew within the middle classes that the working classes were using their leisure time in ways that were not conducive to their own well-being or that of society.

There was also great concern in the middle of the 18th century that Britain was falling behind Europe in terms of its provision of libraries freely accessible for the general public. The notion of large cities providing an accessible collection of books for the general public was common in Europe, with Italy, France and Germany all leading the way in provision (Minto, 1932, 80). As will be seen below, these points were made prominently in the evidence gathered by the Select Committee examining the need for an Act of Parliament related to public libraries.

A precursor to the 1850 Act was the 1835 attempt by John Silk Buckingham to present a Public Institutions Bill, aimed at allowing local boroughs to levy a tax to create museums and libraries; however, this failed to reach the statute books. Buckingham was an advocate of temperance, and wished to create spaces other than public houses for workers to frequent in their leisure time, thus his ideas incorporated not only the creation of libraries, but also other public spaces supported by the local community.

However, Buckingham's efforts influenced two of the leading figures in the path towards the 1850 Act, MPs William Ewart and Joseph Brotherton. The initial success of the pair came with the passing of the 1845 Museums Act which 'empowered boroughs with a population of 10,000 or more to raise a ½ d rate for the establishment of museums' (Kelly and Kelly, 1977, 77). This Act can be seen as a major influence in the road to a Public Libraries Act. The pair later joined forces with an assistant at the then British Museum Library, Edward Edwards, who had previously published pamphlets on the potential of public libraries to enhance communities. Edwards was 'a self taught former bricklayer . . . passionately convinced of the value and significance of libraries' (Sturges, 1996, 30).

Their efforts in advocacy paid off in 1849 with the formation of a Select Committee charged with investigating the state of free public library provision. Ewart and Brotherton became members of the Select Committee, and Edward Edwards was a key witness before it, 'and, very naturally, his message was that public libraries were conducive to the development of a better educated and better informed populace' (Sturges, 1996, 30).

Moving to the Act

The Select Committee of Parliament charged with gathering evidence for evaluating the 'best Means of Extending the establishment of LIBRARIES freely open to the Public, especially in large towns, in Great Britain and Ireland' began its deliberations in March 1849. The opening paragraphs of the Select Committee Report lament the fact that the great scholars of the time who hailed from Britain were very often challenged in their work by limited access to scholarly works. While bemoaning the fact that historians such as Gibbons, Roscoe and Graham were unable to satisfy their research needs in British libraries, it suggested that their foreign counterparts were not so disadvantaged: 'While we learn that, more than half a century ago, the first step taken by a foreign writer was to consult a Public Library on the subject of his studies or composition; we find that no such auxiliary was at the service of the British intellect' (House of Commons, 1849, iii).

The Committee's final report ran to 450 pages of passionate evidence extolling the virtues of public libraries in large towns and cities, and constantly reinforcing the benefits continental Europeans enjoyed that their British counterparts did not. Statistics were presented showing that the major cities of Britain's European rivals contained several publicly accessible libraries, with seven in Paris, four in Dresden, two in Berlin, three in Vienna and six in Florence (House of Commons, 1849, iv). The statistics for the countries as a whole were even starker, with France attributed with 107 libraries, Prussia 44, Austria 48 and Bavaria 17.

The report was also at pains to suggest the social transformation that could occur with the provision of a library service. Citing the example of Peebles Library in Scotland it suggested that the library had 'promoted literary taste and temperate and moral habits among the inhabitants' (House of Commons, 1849, vii). Another benefit that would be accrued from the formation of public libraries, it was argued, would revolve around steering the public away from frivolous or immoral works of literature: 'It is also truly observed that the establishment of such depositories of standard literature would lessen, or perhaps entirely destroy, the influence of frivolous, unsound or dangerous works' (House of Commons, 1849, viii). In closing this argument the question is asked: 'Shall we therefore abandon the people to the influence of a low, enfeebling, and often pestilential literature, instead of enabling them to breathe a more elevated, and more congenial atmosphere?'(House of Commons, 1849, vii).

Even with the 450-page report produced by the Select Committee, the Bill did not receive an easy ride through Parliament. Objections were in several areas. Some MPs objected to the tax-based element of the proposals, but others objected to the potential for lecture rooms in the libraries to lead to increased social agitation if they were used for political purposes (Kelly and Kelly, 1977, 80).

The Public Libraries Bill was presented to Parliament in February 1850, and became law with the granting of Royal Assent in August of the same year. The provisions of the Act were that town councils administering over a population of more than 10,000 people were now able to levy a half-penny rate to provide the accommodation for and maintenance of a library and/or museum (Kelly, 1977, 15). Crucially, however, the tax could only be levied for the provision of the library building, its upkeep, and to hire staff. It could not be used to buy library materials such as the books necessary to lend to the public, for which the library would have to rely on the philanthropy of the local community. For a town to adopt the Act, the question of whether to support a public library had to be put to a vote of the people and a two-thirds majority received in favour of the motion. The 1850 Act applied only to towns in England and Wales, and thus in the summer of 1853 an Act was passed that extended the provisions of the 1850 Act to Scotland and Ireland.

Early public library development

The same arguments against the merits of the Act were used by objectors within the local communities themselves when charged with voting for the creation of a library. In Scotland, Edinburgh and Glasgow notably resisted early adoption of public libraries, and in England the proposal was rejected on more than one occasion by several boroughs, including Islington, Bath and Hull (Kelly and Kelly, 1977, 81).

Norwich, continuing its leadership in such things from the 17th century, was the first local council to adopt the Act with a vote of 150 for the motion, and only seven against, although due to the ambition of the project they instigated the service did not open until 1857 (Minto, 1932, 96). The first public library to open under the auspices of the Act was in Winchester, which adopted and opened the service in 1851 (Kelly and Kelly, 1977, 88). Edward Edwards returned to prominence in 1852 as the librarian of the first large municipal library adopted under the Act, in Manchester. The opening of the library was a stellar affair, with orators present including Dickens and Thackeray (Kelly and Kelly, 1977, 89).

However, early take up of the Act was generally poor, especially in London, which was ironically one of the main urban targets of the legislation in the first place. Even over 30 years after the first Public Libraries Act, there was no real national network to speak of. A Parliamentary return in 1885 indicated that only 23% of the British population were served by a public library, 23% in England, 15% in Wales, and only 8% in Scotland (Kelly, 1977, 122). Many arguments have been posited as to why this was the case, and Sykes suggests that the very notion of the free library rather than being a selling point was actually a negative in the minds of many potential users. He argues that 'In appearance, location and smell many were associated with that very condition so abhorred by the bulk of the working class – charity' (Sykes, 1979, 19). Sykes goes on to suggest that the 1850 Act was introduced too early and that a more successful outcome would have occurred had it been introduced 20 years later (19).

Yet despite this, by the end of the First World War, the number of public libraries had risen significantly to 602, from a number totalling 125 in 1886 (Kelly, 1977, 122). The 1850 Act was amended several times over the succeeding decades, most notably to incorporate changes to the population levels where they could be created (reduced to 5000 in 1855 and removed entirely in 1866) and to raise the levy to one penny. This legislation, while on paper enhancing the number of towns and villages able to adopt a public library, also led to many communities creating them that simply did not have the population to sustain them in a fit state.

The penny rate, which it has been argued 'did more to retard the progress of public libraries than anything else' (Minto, 1932, 125), was finally abolished with the passing of the 1919 Public Libraries Act. This Act was a significant influence on the network of public libraries, for other reasons:

- It allowed county councils to establish library services across their entire geographic domain.
- It permitted existing town libraries to hand over their administration to the local authority.

As a result many small libraries that had existed solely under the funding of their local community, and in isolation, became part of a local network of libraries. Thus the 1919 Act was a first step towards a professionally managed national network. However, it was not the panacea for the problems of variance in service provision across the country, and it was not until the McColvin Report (discussed below) that the inadequacies were widely debated.

Philanthropy and growth

As significant a figure as anyone in terms of the development of public libraries was the industrialist Andrew Carnegie. A Scottish-born émigré who made his wealth in the steel industry in Philadelphia, he spent a large portion of his fortune in philanthropic works, and his investment in public libraries in North America, Britain, Australia and New Zealand transformed the lives of many communities through his Carnegie Trust. He explained in his inimitable style why he chose to spend his fortune in this way: 'No millionaire will go wrong in his search for one of the best forms for the use of his surplus who chooses to establish a free library in any community that is willing to maintain and develop it' (Carnegie quoted in Aitken, 1971, 76).

Some of the sums allocated to communities to build libraries were significant, even by standards of today. The exercise began in Carnegie's hometown of Dunfermline where an £8000 grant was provided to create a free library, which opened in 1883. In total, throughout the world,

Carnegie's generosity funded the development of some 3000 libraries, an incredible gift to humanity. As well as this influence, the Carnegie Trust also funded research into library use with its 1915 study into the position of public libraries in England and Wales. The Trust was also a major catalyst in promoting interlibrary co-operation and lending through the funding of regional catalogue development.

Other philanthropists were significant contributors to the advancement of public libraries in Britain. John Passmore Edwards was central to the development of libraries in London and Cornwall, and in Glasgow, as previously discussed, a notable contribution was made by tobacco baron Stephen Mitchell who bequeathed a gift to the city that resulted in the development of the Mitchell Library. Many of the finest and oldest public library buildings in the UK owe their existence to the philanthropic gestures of others. The investment in public library buildings in the late Victorian and early Edwardian period went a long way to installing the infrastructure we now take for granted.

The McColvin Report and post-war developments

The publication of *The Public Library System of Great Britain*, or the McColvin Report, as it came to be known, set the case for a realignment of public library services. The report was published in 1942 and attacked the variance in quality of library services across the country, with particular emphasis on rural libraries. McColvin was highly critical of what he saw as a fragmented structure, and he advocated larger administrative units being constructed to look after multiple libraries, a reduction from 604 library authorities UK wide, to just 93 (McColvin, 1942, 149-57). This was a crucial point, as the variances in quality and service were inevitable with the huge differences in populations served by libraries; while some served populations in the thousands, others like metropolitan services had to cater for numbers in excess of a million. McColvin's belief was that only large structures could deliver the range of services modern libraries were required to provide for their users, such as children's services, and efficient and effective reference services. Indeed, in terms of reference services it became clear that the large city authorities began to develop some outstanding provision in this area due to their size and organization, with several including Manchester, Glasgow and Liverpool developing superb collections of journals and reference materials that smaller authorities could not replicate. This led to many of the major city reference libraries serving not only as reference hubs for their own community, but also being called on by smaller authorities to answer questions when their own resources could not meet the needs of users.

McColvin's goal, however, was not a navel-gazing lament for the current inadequacies, but a focus on what the future could be for the public library service, and a call for central government to play its part in the funding of libraries by the provision of grants. He was a believer in the potential of the public library service to transform communities if properly delivered and managed, and this passion was evident in his report as he considered what he believed to be unacceptable variances in quality throughout the UK.

The report was not only an overview of the current state of play in libraries, but also a motivating tool for a generation of librarians. As Black has suggested, this idealistic report 'resurrected the burning faith in the importance of self-realisation through the public library which had marked the discourses of the service's Victorian pioneers' (Black, 2000, 97). Published as it was during the Second World War the report hit a note within a society ready for radical change post-war, the kind of radical change that brought about a transformation to a Labour government, and the development of the National Health Service. Public libraries became, if not a major strand of the emerging welfare state, a large-scale example of the principles of welfarism (Black, 2000, 111).

In his exhaustive consideration of the impact of the report Whiteman concludes that its central message 'remains of long-term significance' (1986, 181). For him the key legacies of the report are its focus on the transformational qualities of the public library for its citizens, and its notion that only large, well organized authorities can deliver the range of services necessary.

McColvin also discussed the nature of the workforce of the public library, advocating a more formal approach to the training and qualifications of librarians serving in the public sector. The qualifications for librarians were administered by The Library Association (LA), formed in 1877. Perhaps the most pivotal moment in the LA's early history was the receipt of its Royal Charter in 1898, which gave it status as the 'supreme arbiter of all matters concerned with professional library practice' but also crucially gave the Association sole responsibility:

■   to promote whatever tends to the improvement of the position and qualifications for librarians
■   to hold examinations in librarianship and to issue certificates of efficiency.

(Bramley, 1981, 29)

McColvin proposed a two-tier category for library staff, namely professional and non-professional. Professional staff would preferably be university graduates, but would at least bear the Higher School Certificate. Progression to professional librarian status would be related to applicants successfully undertaking a two-year full-time course at an authorized library school (Whiteman, 1986, 97). On consideration of the recommendations, the LA proposed a set of criteria that largely mirrored those set out by McColvin, although graduate entry was played down somewhat more than in the original report. A key strategy of the McColvin and LA approaches was the establishment of a network of library schools covering the country, and this was perhaps the most crucial catalyst in moving librarianship to a graduate profession, with the explosion in numbers in the late 1960s onwards and the recognition by the late 1970s that the majority of new entrants to the library profession were now coming via the graduate route, leading to a re-evaluation of the LA's qualifications system to assert that the minimum requirement for entry to the professional register was a degree or equivalent .

The modern statutory context

The most significant development in the later part of the 20th century was the adoption of a new Act of Parliament for libraries, the 1964 Public Libraries and Museums Act, which came into force in April 1965. The most important component of this Act was that it made it a statutory obligation for a local authority to provide a 'comprehensive and efficient' public library service for its community. With this came the power of the Secretary of State to oversee library services, and 'superintend' their operations. A dramatic aspect of the Act was in the aforementioned powers it conferred on the Secretary of State to remove the right to be a library authority from any service deemed to be unacceptable in its performance. The Act made clear, however, that this was a scenario that should only take place in the most extreme circumstances.

The Act also led to the formation of library advisory councils for England and Wales, which still exist to this day. In England the advisory council is now in the form of the Museums, Libraries and Archives Council, or MLA. The MLA (2008) describes its role as follows:

> We deliver strategic leadership in England and in each of its regions and we collaborate with partners across the UK. Our research identifies good practice, which we use to promote improvement. We offer advice, support and resources to funding bodies and other groups to incentivise innovation. Our aim is to raise professional standards and champion better services for users and readers of all ages and backgrounds, whether residents or visitors.

The MLA through its policy remit provides regular reports and funds research into aspects of public library services, several of which are discussed in more detail in Chapter 1.

These developments led to a national strategic framework for public libraries as well as providing national standards that librarians could use to measure their service quality against. This Act remains the statutory framework for the delivery of library services in England and Wales.

Local government reorganization

Local government reorganization in the early 1970s and mid 1990s has also had a significant impact on the way public library services have been delivered. We will discuss local authority governance and reorganization in detail in Chapter 8, but the key issues to bear in mind throughout the discussions in the following chapters relate to the impacts any iteration of local authority reorganization has on the structure of the service, namely:

- *change in the geographic region the library authority serves*: this often means that after reorganization, specific libraries find themselves part of a new geographic grouping; for instance in the 1996 reorganization in Scotland, Glasgow City Council had its geographic boundaries redrawn, and several libraries were transferred to the new South Lanarkshire Council
- *change in the departmental structure of the local authorities*: in recent reorganizations, departments have been merged together for multiple services. Therefore it is now uncommon to find a department solely responsible for libraries; they would now often find themselves part of a larger department with overall responsibility for services as diverse as theatres, museums, libraries, education or community services.

The implications of these changes will be discussed more fully in Chapter 8.

Conclusion

We can see that the development of public libraries in the UK has been a case of historical trial and error, founded on the good will and commitment of many individuals and communities to arrive at a national model for delivery, and an expectation of service quality that is broadly universal. Essentially the 1850 Act rather than create a brand new network from scratch actually led to the formalization of a pre-existing network of ad hoc libraries which were added to as the public library concept gained ground.

The public library network that remains in the UK continues to be strong in numbers, with over 4500 public libraries when last counted (CILIP, 2007). It remains a significant investment for the public purse to fund them. Despite the controversies and challenges faced by the institutions, we can look back at the work of reformers such as Ewart, Brotherton and Edwards and acknowledge that their vision, which started small, has become a project of immense national pride. The modern, nationally accountable, professionally run network of public libraries would have been far beyond the visions of the early campaigners. McColvin has suggested that the most important aspect of the work of the reformers was that they inspired five key principles on which our modern understanding of public libraries is now enshrined:

- that public libraries should be publicly funded
- that they should be administered by public bodies and not private organizations or individuals
- that they should be freely available to all members of the community
- that they should embrace the needs and interest of all members of the community
- that they should be free both financially and intellectually, and provide access to materials without bias or interference.

(McColvin, 1956, 24)

These principles underlie the basis of the modern public library service; however, as will be seen in later chapters they are principles that have frequently come under challenge.

The next part of the book relates to the services of the modern public library discussed under four distinct categories: equity of access, cultural and leisure roles, information and informed citizenship, and lifelong learning.

References

Aitken, W. R. (1971) *A History of the Public Library Movement in Scotland to 1955*, Scottish Library Association.

Black, A. (1996) *A New History of the English Public Library: social and intellectual contexts, 1850-1914*, Leicester University Press.

Black, A. (2000) *The Public Library in Britain 1914-2000*, The British Library.

Bramley, G. (1981) *Apprentice to Graduate: a history of library education in the United Kingdom*, Clive Bingley.

CILIP (2007) How Many Libraries Are There in the UK?, www.cilip.org.uk/informationadvice/services/numberoflibraries. htm.

Gray, D. (1949) The Public Library Makes a Century, *Library Review*, **12** (2), 83-6.

Greenwood, T. G. (1891) *Public Libraries: a history of the movement and a manual for the organization and management of rate supported libraries*, Cassell & Company.

Hendry, J. D. (1974) *A Social History of Branch Library Development: with special reference to the City of Glasgow*, Scottish Library Association.

House of Commons (1849) *Report of the Select Committee on Public Libraries Together with the Minutes of Evidence and Appendix*, House of Commons.

Kelly, T. (1966) *Public Libraries in Great Britain before 1850*, Library Association.

Kelly, T. (1977) *History of Public Libraries in Great Britain 1845-1975*, Library Association.

Kelly, T. and Kelly, E. (1977) *Books for the People: an illustrated history of the British public library*, Andre Deutsch.

Kent, A. et al. (1978) *Encyclopedia of Library and Information Science*, vol. 24, Marcel Dekker.

McColvin, L. (1942) *The Public Library System of Great Britain*, Library Association.

McColvin, L. (1956) *The Chance to Read: public libraries in the world today*, Phoenix House.

Minto, J. (1932) *A History of the Public Library Movement in Great Britain and Ireland*, George Allen & Unwin and The Library Association.

MLA (2008) *MLA - About Us*, www.mla.gov.uk/aboutus/.

Murison, W. J. (1971) *The Public Library*, 2nd edn, George G. Harrap.

Sturges, P. (1996) Conceptualizing the Public Library 1850-1919. In Kinnell, M. and Sturges, P. (eds), *Continuity and Innovation in the Public Library: the development of a social institution*, Library Association.

Sykes, P. (1979) *The Public Library in Perspective: an examination of its origins and modern role*, Clive Bingley.

Whiteman, P. (1986) *Public Libraries Since 1945: the impact of the McColvin Report*, Clive Bingley.

Part 2

Service themes of the modern public library

Chapter 3

Equity of access

Introduction

Rather than merely being described as a service theme, providing equity of access could also be defined as a core mission for public libraries and, as discussed in Chapter 2, is one of the key reasons why public libraries were formed in the first place. Equity of access is about all members of a community having the right to use the information and books that they need regardless of their ability to afford them or without undue influence or prejudice from others who may wish them not to have access.

The right for anyone of any race, creed or colour to access the collected knowledge of humankind is something that it is easy to take for granted, but ultimately that is the key role of the public library for its community. This is a key strand of the joint *IFLA/UNESCO Public Library Manifesto*, which states that 'services of the public library are provided on the basis of equality of access for all, regardless of age, race, sex, religion, nationality, language or social status' (IFLA, 2004).

Therefore, although all of the service themes we will discuss in the following chapters fit the notion of equity of access, this chapter will focus solely on:

- the broad notion of equity and freedom of access as a core mission of public libraries
- the professional challenges faced by the librarian in providing equity of access
- services aimed at specific user communities to facilitate equity of access.

Core values

Librarians pride themselves on working in a profession that is happy to serve all library patrons, and defend their right to access materials. This is enshrined in the professional codes of many of the associations that represent librarians across the world (ALA, 1995; ALIA, 2005; CILIP, 2005).

Writings on library values

Over the years attempts have been made to provide a core set of values for the profession of librarianship, and the concept of providing equity of access features prominently. The first major set of values set out were the *Five Laws of Library Science* espoused in 1931 by S. R. Ranganathan:

1   Books are for use.
2   For every reader, his or her book.
3   For every book, its reader.
4   Save the time of the reader.
5   A library is a growing organism.   (Ranganathan, 1931)

While the terminology could be seen as historically grounded the principles provided are as relevant today as they were in 1931. Ranganathan has been interpreted exhaustively over the years since his five laws were first published, but a simple translation of them for the modern era might be:

1   We must encourage all potential users to access information.
2   Regardless of creed or colour there is something a library has that will be of value to a user.
3   We must ensure that the way we organize and store the material is for the benefit of the user and not our own.

4   We should continuously add to the collections we make available to
     people and manage this accordingly.

At the heart of Ranganathan's laws are the universal notions of there being
equity of access to, and availability of, information for all.

In recent years Michael Gorman has made an attempt to revisit the
guiding principles and values of librarianship; he has identified eight
themes that he calls the enduring values, namely:

- stewardship
- service
- intellectual freedom
- equity of access
- privacy
- literacy and learning
- rationalism
- democracy.   (Gorman, 2000)

Gorman's ethos mirrors that of Ranganathan, yet he articulates a fuller set
of principles for the modern era. The themes of intellectual freedom and
rationalism play to a world where both are continuously under threat.
Gorman's values are interesting because they combine a twin track of
service delivery and professional influence; not merely the act of issuing
a book or a piece of information, but knowing that, by doing so, you are
contributing to a larger goal, be it the literacy of the individual, the
intellectual freedom of the author, or the rationalism of society fighting
against censorship.

The values and principles espoused by Gorman and Ranganathan
can be seen as central to the public library mission. In the specific context
of public libraries, Usherwood has recently revisited the issue of equity
from the point of view of his belief that services should be focusing on a
breadth of material, to include both popular and high quality literature,
in order to achieve equity of access (Usherwood, 2007).

Public library as social equalizer

The public library acts as a social equalizer by providing the public with access to books and information, which many people cannot afford to buy themselves. It would be expensive for voracious readers who borrow several titles per week if they chose to purchase them. Yet with the public library on their doorstep they can borrow titles without worrying about the expense.

Crucially the same applies to access to expensive items of information, such as encyclopedias and other reference materials. Many of the best and most respected reference sources are truly only within the buying power of large institutions like libraries, and without them purchasing such materials for users it would be difficult for someone who could not afford the expense to be able to access these works.

Prejudice free

The selection of materials for users must be free from any bias or prejudice on the part of the librarian or others, if they are undertaking selection on the librarian's behalf. This is all the more vital when dealing with viewpoints from communities that may differ, since often religious and ethnic tension can lead to controversy in terms of specific texts or themes present in texts. The public library must offer a balanced collection that takes into account all viewpoints, even those that may be controversial or challenge orthodoxy. Not to do so limits the potential reach of the library, and perhaps more importantly the ability of the users to broaden their horizons.

Independence of selection

This brings us to the issue of independence of selection. A fundamental role of the librarian is to ensure that selection of materials is undertaken with the wider interests and needs of the community they serve in mind.

Clearly it is a positive policy to allow library users to request material to be purchased, and this is a common feature of all libraries; however, the purchasing decision should be made independently by the librarian, to ensure:

- the library obtains value for money
- the purchase is appropriate.

Titles requested may be overly expensive or may not meet the needs of the community in other ways, and the librarian is charged with making this decision in the best interests of the community.

Public library as historical archive

Although it is not the statutory obligation of the public library to operate in the same capacity as a national library and gather the totality of experience and printed works produced in a specific country, in many large library authorities the central reference library operates as a de facto regional library, collecting important materials and building special collections of crucial local and regional importance. In addition local branch libraries may well hold in their own local history collections material of a rare if not commercially valuable nature. It is important that this type of material is preserved for future generations, and thus public libraries must maintain a store where older material can be housed safely.

Breadth of choice

An ongoing concern for librarians should be the goal of ensuring that users have access to as broad a range of material as is practicable. This is not always straightforward, however. For instance, a limited budget can provide challenges for librarians who have the twin pressures of purchasing enough in-demand material to satisfy user requests while also ensuring that they build a collection that is representative of the cultural, educational and leisure needs of the community. This tension increases more in an environment where performance of the library is measured in terms of the number of book issues it can deliver. The temptation may be to buy material that is popular to ensure usage figures are robust. This tension of how to measure services appropriately will be discussed in more detail in Chapter 9.

Censorship

Censorship is an affront to a democratic nation and something that library associations across the world attempt to combat through their ethical policies, adhered to by members. It can take several forms, from subtle pressure not to purchase material on a certain topic or by certain authors, to more overt campaigns by special interest groups or individuals within a community who wish their own moral viewpoint to be at the fore.

Censorship can also involve self censorship, where a librarian errs on the side of caution so as not to offend or potentially make available material that may be illegal. Such an occurrence is not alien to the UK, as for 15 years between 1988 and 2003 (2000 in Scotland) it was illegal for a local authority to promote homosexuality. The specific law, Section 28 of the Local Government Act 1988, stated that a local authority 'shall not intentionally promote homosexuality or publish material with the intention of promoting homosexuality', which led to confusion among librarians as to what could be purchased, and to subsequent problems in collection development for materials of interest to the gay and lesbian community. Clearly while the librarian risked breaking the law by purchasing some material that dealt with gay and lesbian issues as a result of such a draconian piece of legislation, fear of doing so led to some self censorship and erring on the side of caution, to the detriment of collection building and providing an equal service to a large number of users.

Self censorship can also occur for political reasons. In 1986 a bitter industrial dispute occurred between News International and the print trade unions, and as a result between 20 and 30 public library authorities, including those in major cities such as Glasgow, Edinburgh and Sheffield, refused to display copies of any newspapers published by News International (Ezard, 1986). Such a stance, while politically expedient for the political party in control of the public library service, is an affront to the notion of equity of access. It was also later deemed illegal in court in 1987 when in the case R vs. *London Borough of Ealing and others ex parte Times Newspapers* it was deemed to be an unlawful abuse of the 1964 Public Libraries Act because the decision was made purely on politics.

In the USA the American Library Association (ALA) has operated an annual Banned Books week since 1982 to draw attention to censorship across the country in libraries of all kinds (www.ala.org/bbooks/). As part of the campaign they issue a list of the most challenged books in the preceding year; these are the books most complained about by patrons, or books that receive requests to be removed from shelves for political, religious or moral reasons. The top five titles in 2007 with reasons why they were challenged were:

- *And Tango Makes Three*, by Justin Richardson and Peter Parnell. Reasons: anti-ethnic, sexism, homosexuality, anti-family, religious viewpoint, unsuited to age group
- *The Chocolate War*, by Robert Cormier. Reasons: sexually explicit, offensive language, violence
- *Olive's Ocean*, by Kevin Henkes. Reasons: sexually explicit, offensive language
- *The Golden Compass*, by Philip Pullman. Reasons: religious viewpoint
- *The Adventures of Huckleberry Finn*, by Mark Twain. Reasons: racism. (Source: www.ala.org/bbooks/)

The title that is number one on the list deals with the story of two male penguins that take on the parenting of an egg from a mixed sex couple, and clearly would be controversial for some who are against same sex partnerships or same sex couples looking after children. Although recent titles such as *And Tango Makes Three* are prominent in the list, classical books such as *The Adventures of Huckleberry Finn* also feature prominently. It must be noted that censorship is not only the domain of what could be perceived to be the reactionary elements in society; some groups who class themselves as liberal also call for censorship, with *The Adventures of Huckleberry Finn* being a case in point as it is challenged as a title based on perceived racism within its pages.

Hate on the state

Thus libraries have to be accountable for the stock they purchase on behalf of their users. They can do this formally by adopting collection development policies, a topic that will be discussed in more detail in Chapter 4.

A recent case where accountability for stock selection was challenged was the recent *Hate on the State* report (Brandon and Murray, 2007) published in August 2007 by the Centre for Social Cohesion. The report centred on the availability of what was deemed to be extremist Islamic materials in several UK public libraries. The charges against the books in question were that they:

- glorify acts of terrorism against followers of other religions
- incite violence against anyone who rejects jihadist ideologies
- endorse violence and discrimination against women.

(Brandon and Murray, 2007, 3)

These were clearly issues that the public should be made aware of, but the report continued that it was not merely the existence of the books, but the fact that libraries were actively promoting their availability to users, that was of concern:

In a number of cases these books are not only on library shelves but are also given special prominence in displays. Such books abuse traditions of rationalism and tolerance and risk damaging community cohesion. In the worst cases they are the tools of radicalisation and increase the risk of Islamic terrorism.

(Brandon and Murray, 2007, 3)

Although the points made in much of the report could be deemed to be exacerbated by contemporaneous concerns with Islamic terrorism, the key issue for the library profession came in the arguments raised regarding balanced collections. The authors argued that:

- Any member of the public who wanted to learn about Islam and who visited these libraries with no prior knowledge would be led to believe that the most extreme interpretations of the religion, extolling bigotry, separatism and even violence, are the most legitimate and commonplace.
- A reader who was already Muslim or who was interested in adopting Islam as a religion – if relying on such books – would also be pushed towards the most radical and political interpretations of Islam.

■   Any Muslim citizen who is already influenced by radical Islam can 'top
     up' on radical literature in state-owned and state-funded institutions.
                                                  (Brandon and Murray, 2007, 3)

It is difficult to argue with the logic inherent in these points. Undoubtedly
the collections in public libraries should offer appropriate balance and the
report made for some negative publicity for the library authorities
concerned. However, in comments to the press regarding the report the
Chartered Institute of Library and Information Professionals (CILIP)
and Tower Hamlets Council reinforced the importance of public libraries
offering a breadth of material, even controversial material, to library
users.

Despite the UK and USA being two of the foremost liberal democracies
in the world, cries to restrict access to or ban altogether material deemed
objectionable can and do occur. It is therefore important that both as
individual authorities and as a wider profession public librarians are
aware of such calls and able to address them proactively. As the ALA has
reported, the majority of challenges to material go unreported, and as a
result the decisions on whether to restrict or ban also go unreported. Since
the UK has no equivalent of Banned Books week it is difficult to estimate
how large a problem this is, but the rise in influence and the resultant
lobbying of religious and other special interest groups raises the potential
for material to be challenged. IFLA's Committee on Free Access to
Information and Freedom of Expression (FAIFE) has a website
(www.ifla.org/faife/) offering advice and resources on intellectual freedom
including policy documents, which may be useful in such cases.

There are also specific issues related to public access computing that
pose significant challenges to public librarians, such as privacy and
filtering; these will be discussed in detail in Chapter 7.

Enabling equitable access to materials

Facilitating access to library materials involves a process of procurement,
processing and then making material available. Collection development
policies will be discussed in detail in the next chapter; however, the
keystone in providing equitable access to library materials is the library

catalogue, and thus the quality and consistency of cataloguing and classification used within the library.

Organization and cataloguing

Like all other types of library, public libraries collect materials and organize them. Efficient organization of the materials is vital, since library users must be able to retrieve them easily and with minimum effort. The challenge for the public library is to ensure that they use a system of organization that is efficient enough to aid retrieval for all members of the public, but robust enough to ensure materials are arranged logically and to a system of recognizable professional competency. An overly complex system can be confusing for a library user; however, a system that is too simplistic can be equally confusing if it means categories or classifications assigned to items are too broad.

Most public libraries in the UK use the Dewey Decimal Classification system for organizing materials, in which each item is classified with a number that denotes a subject. However, since many Dewey categories involve many numbers after the decimal point, public libraries often use a simplified form of the classification, with only four or five numbers after the point. Although this system may not be technically correct, it offers a simplified system for the library user to access the material.

Making materials available

Public libraries provide open access for the most part. Clearly while there will always be too many books in the system to display on the shelves, library staff attempt to make the material that is on open access circulate as much as is practicable. This is a key aspect of providing equity of access, allowing library users to browse the shelves and select material for themselves without having to seek access through the librarian.

Often large reference libraries can only keep a limited number of items on open access due to the size of their collections. In such cases having a good supply of online public access catalogues (OPACs) is crucial to allow users to browse the catalogue quickly. Regular weeding of material on open access is also important in reference libraries to ensure that the most up to date and relevant materials are available for users.

Social inclusion

Perhaps the term that most librarians in the modern era would equate with equity of access is the phrase social inclusion. This term has gained prominence in the UK since the election of the New Labour Government in 1997. Early in its tenure it set up a Social Exclusion Unit, which in 2006 became the Social Exclusion Task Force based in the Cabinet Office. The remit of the Task Force is to focus on the most excluded people in society and ensure different government departments and other agencies work together to facilitate inclusion. The Social Exclusion Task Force defines social exclusion as:

> a short-hand term for what can happen when people or areas have a combination of linked problems, such as unemployment, discrimination, poor skills, low incomes, poor housing, high crime and family breakdown. These problems are linked and mutually reinforcing. Social exclusion is an extreme consequence of what happens when people don't get a fair deal throughout their lives, often because of disadvantage they face at birth, and this disadvantage can be transmitted from one generation to the next.
>
> (Cabinet Office, 2008)

However, social exclusion is about more than income, crime or education levels; it also relates to other barriers to accessing public services, such as geographical or physical barriers. For instance, the challenge of delivering services to people in rural communities is ongoing, as in some cases local authorities cover geographic areas that span huge distances. Getting services to the people in these communities and to users with disabilities is a major challenge.

Social inclusion and public libraries

As public libraries seek to serve all members of society, they have an important role in facilitating social inclusion. In 1999 the Department for Culture, Media and Sport published *Libraries for All: social inclusion in public libraries,* a policy document that gave public libraries a key role in the Government's bid to combat social exclusion. In doing so it identified specific aspects of current service provision that would need to be addressed, and thus made the following recommendations:

1   Social inclusion should be mainstreamed as a policy priority within all library and information services.
2   Library authorities should consider what specific services need to be tailored to meet the needs of minority groups and communities.
3   Library authorities should consult and involve socially excluded groups in order to ascertain their needs and aspirations.
4   Libraries should be located where there is a demand, but should build upon existing facilities and services wherever possible.
5   Opening hours should be more flexible and tailored to reflect the needs and interests of the community.
6   Library and information services should develop their role as community resource centres, providing access to communication as well as information.
7   Library authorities should consider the possibilities of co-locating their facilities with other services provided by the local authority.
8   Libraries should be the local learning place and champion of the independent learner.
9   Libraries should be a major vehicle for providing affordable (or preferably free) access to ICT at local level.
10 Library and information services should form partnerships with other learning organisations.
11 Library authorities should consider whether some services aimed at socially excluded people might be more effectively delivered on a regional basis.

(DCMS, 1999)

This document clearly put the public library front and centre as a facilitator of the Government's social inclusion agenda, and offered enormous opportunities to put public libraries at the political centre once again as an important social influence on the community.

Open to All?

For an 18-month period between October 1998 and April 2000 a major research project was undertaken into how public libraries were contributing towards social inclusion. The findings of the resulting report *Open to All?* suggested that in a bid to be equitable, and having a 'take it or leave it' approach to service provision where excluded people were given only the same consideration as all other users, libraries were failing to achieve social inclusion (Muddiman et al., 2000).

The authors proposed that all levels of stakeholders needed to be more proactive in their approach to addressing exclusion, with specific programmes aimed at excluded communities. The public library would need to become 'a far more proactive and interventionist institution' than it had been to achieve this (Muddiman et al., 2000, 59).

Public libraries and empathy

A recent major study funded by the Arts and Humanities Research Council and undertaken by a team at the Centre for the Public Library and Information in Society at the University of Sheffield investigated public library staff attitudes in England towards social inclusion policies and towards disadvantaged communities (Wilson and Birdi, 2008). The findings 'revealed a lack of clarity and understanding within public library services of what social exclusion means and its relationship with other social policy objectives, particularly within the access and equality agendas' (Wilson and Birdi, 2008, 105). In addition while 50% of respondents to a survey indicated that they were familiar with national social inclusion policy, the qualitative data gathered by the researchers suggested that the real figure was much lower.

The research also revealed tensions within the public library system towards social inclusion policies, with a culture evident of a quick-fix approach to achieving targets in the area (Wilson and Birdi, 2008, 105). The researchers suggested major improvements in recruitment, training and partnership working with appropriate stakeholders where necessary to plug the gaps that existed. Crucially they reiterated the point that a one-size-fits-all approach does not aid inclusion, just as Muddiman et al. reported in 2000.

It would seem then that while public libraries have a clear identification with a mission towards social inclusion, research indicates that much work remains to be done to ensure this is the case.

Public library users

As discussed, public libraries are charged with serving every member of the community. This is a challenging goal for any service, public or private, as to meet the needs of an entire community means being able to satisfy a myriad of diverse user needs and demands.

Let us consider in more detail the broad categories of users a public library strives to serve, and some service scenarios that may be appropriate for that user type:

■ *Children and young people*: services aimed at children and young people are some of the most vital provided by public library services across the world. Specific initiatives will be discussed in more detail in Chapter 4. The emphasis is on encouraging a reading habit within children from an extremely young age, and to develop their reading as they grow up.

■ *Students*: while students are normally well served by the library of the institution they study in, public libraries are expected to provide services for any potential user who lives, works or studies in the area. This means that they must be responsive to the needs of the student population as much as is practicable. In a university town or city served by a public library this could mean a considerable user population whose needs must be understood and met where possible.

■ *Unemployed adults*: the range of services that an unemployed adult may wish to access in their library is wide. As well as the traditional services on offer, such users may seek access to the newspapers for job advertisements, any training or classes on offer within the library premises, and any outreach programmes from other bodies looking to link the unemployed with external opportunities.

- *Working adults*: it could be said that reaching working adults is one of the most challenging aspects of public librarianship. Many adults who work cannot fit their life around the opening hours of their local public library. This raises issues for libraries who see a potentially large swathe of the population that they find difficulty in reaching.
- *Adults with disabilities*: the key considerations in providing services to people with disabilities are related to access to the library building and the materials within. The wider challenges of aged library buildings will be discussed in more detail in Chapter 11; however, with relation to access to the library for disabled users the requirements are not merely a matter of a moral duty to provide access, there is now a legal requirement to do so under the auspices of the Disability Discrimination Act (DDA), the most recent iteration of which was passed in the UK in 2005.
- *Senior citizens*: arguably one of the easiest user groups to market to given the high proportion of senior citizens who frequent libraries, yet there is little specific focus on senior citizens as a group with their own special needs. The public library offers enormous potential for senior citizens to engage with the local community through reading groups and other organized events.
- *Community groups*: organizations within the community have a great deal to gain from the public library, and also a great deal to offer in terms of potential partnerships. Community groups can range from senior citizens or youth clubs to voluntary sector organizations, and each has specific needs.
- *Businesses*: public libraries can offer direct access to information that local businesses may find useful for their operations, everything from access to newspapers, information on potential clients to market reports.
- *Schools*: the needs of schools differ from the needs of children as individual library users. While schools may well organize class visits to the library to engage with help for homework and the like it is important that public libraries also treat the child as an individual user and seek to meet their needs outwith those that are educational.
- *Nurseries*: nursery groups are an excellent way of encouraging younger children to read and enjoy the library as a location. Public libraries

can offer local nurseries and playgroups a venue for activities for children that can alleviate the pressures they may have on their facilities.

Reaching excluded users

Targeting services towards specific user demographics poses challenges for library services. As Muddiman et al. state: 'The particular needs of specific excluded social groups and communities are different. It is not possible, in the end, to reduce them and try to find one universal solution for all excluded communities' (Muddiman et al., 2000, 66).

As discussed above, exclusion can encompass physical, social and geographical barriers against access, and some of the specific initiatives employed by public libraries to combat such barriers are discussed below.

Mobile libraries

Mobile libraries are an extremely important tool for reaching excluded communities. Modern vehicles include easy access doorways to enable elderly and less physically agile users to gain access.

Mobile library provision is almost as old a service as public libraries themselves. Orton tells us that the first recorded instance of a service like this was in 1859 in the Northern England town of Warrington when the local mechanics' institute used a horse-drawn van to reach the local working classes with book materials (Orton, 1980, 10).

A modern slant on the mobile library is the ability technology offers to make the vehicles internet-enabled, offering the chance for the communities who use them to take part in the benefits of the People's Network programme. The common solution adopted by library authorities is to use satellite technology on the mobile libraries to enable internet access. This also enhances services by providing real-time catalogue access and data. Previous solutions would either tie the vehicles to a location by using roadside hubs for access, or use mobile phone technologies. The new satellite technologies mean that the mobile libraries can stop anywhere where they have a line of sight to the sky, so vehicles can be much more involved in community events and the like.

Services to ethnic minorities

Public libraries have offered pathways into the social life and culture of Britain for minority communities and immigrants since their inception. Equally they offer the ideal venue for members of ethnic minorities to know that society values their culture through access to works in their mother tongue, or related to their religion or culture.

The role of a librarian supporting ethnic minorities is challenging, since depending on the community there may be numerous languages and cultures. In addition immigration is a fluid process, and with the opening up of European borders to the east, immigrants from the former Soviet republics have moved to the UK in large numbers to find work. As people who live in the community and pay taxes they have a legal and moral right to expect library services be provided for them.

Librarians supporting ethnic minority communities need to build partnerships with community groups and other specialist organizations to ensure they can build collections that represent the cultures of the communities served by the library. They will also be concerned to ensure that as much documentation as practicable is translated for users who do not speak English as a first language.

Asylum seekers and refugees

The Welcome to your Library project was an initiative that ran from 2003 to 2007 and aimed to connect public library services with immigrant and refugee communities. It was funded through the Paul Hamlyn Foundation and co-ordinated through London Libraries Development Agency.

As part of its remit it developed a good practice guide aimed at informing public library staff about the issues inherent in dealing with refugee and asylum seeker communities, and the policies they needed to be aware of in providing services. It also offered advice and contact details for further information on service development for this community (Vincent, 2007).

Services to users with special needs

It is now a legal requirement for public services in the UK to ensure where reasonable that they provide access to services to people with disabilities.

This can be easier said than done in some libraries housed within old buildings that are difficult to make accessible. Physical infrastructure improvements are the most visible way of ensuring disabled users can gain access, including installing ramps for wheelchairs, and perhaps elevators for libraries that have multiple floors.

ICTs bring other challenges, and assistive technologies offer the opportunity to make previously inaccessible ICT-based services accessible to disabled users. There are numerous types of assistive technologies related to several ICT uses, which are discussed below:

- *Pointing devices*: many disabled users have problems navigating a desktop using a traditional mouse. The most common solution to this problem is a tracker ball, which is a large ball housed in a mechanism that allows the full hand to navigate the cursor on screen. This also means that users who have arthritis can also use this instead of a mouse to operate the desktop of the computer.
- *Alternative keyboards*: similarly to the mouse, many disabled users have difficulty using a traditional keyboard. Alternatives exist that provide a solution to this problem. The key element in most alternative keyboards are larger keys, but some use coloured keys as well as using an alternative to the QWERTY key set up. This is normally achieved by simply putting the keys in standard alphabetical order, making the keys easier to find for someone not familiar with QWERTY.
- *Software solutions*: for visually impaired users the problem is reading what is on the screen and also typing text on to the screen. Solutions exist for this, the most famous for screen-reading software being JAWS. JAWS narrates the contents of the screen to the user, even highlighting where an image appears and where a hyperlink appears on a page. The use of such software makes good web page design (see Chapter 5) all the more vital, as sloppily captioned links or images prevent the software from recognizing the image or link for what it is. Speech recognition software can be used to allow the user to dictate to the computer and allow the dictation to be translated into text on the computer screen.

The challenge in the uptake of assistive technologies is in terms of the costs of the solutions. It is common to find only a handful of machines in a library equipped with the technologies necessary, both software and hardware driven. How provision of such technologies is accomplished is obviously a decision for local authorities to consider themselves, but it seems sensible that at least one tracking ball and large keyboard should be available in every public library in the UK.

Housebound services

Housebound services are a crucial tool in facilitating social inclusion of library services. For many citizens who are unable to visit the library in person such services offer an important outlet for them to access reading materials.

The common model is for users to register with the library service and to receive a regular (normally monthly) visit from a volunteer or library staff member who will bring books. Titles are selected according to the responses a user gives on a questionnaire asking about their tastes. Library staff then put together a range of titles for them based on their stated preferences.

Sheffield City Council offers a value-added housebound service that allows users to interact with others via regular newsletters. Users can send the service small items of poetry, book reviews or recipes to share in the newsletters with other users.

Impact of library closures and reduced opening hours

One of the key suggestions from the *Libraries for All* report was that opening hours of libraries should be flexible and meet the needs of the community. Clearly if a library has restricted opening hours it limits the amount of use the community can make of it, and if a library is completely closed it cannot meet its mission to provide equity of access.

The results of an 11 year study of opening hour reductions and closures in libraries in England and Wales are summarized below:

■ *Opening hours*: the researchers found that individual libraries reducing opening hours had a small impact on the community, and some libraries in the case studies suggested that book issues actually rose despite a 30% reduction in opening hours (Proctor, Lee and Reilly, 1998, 85). The researchers were wary of such figures in terms of real impact on the community, and suggested more research was necessary into the many variables that may encourage library users to make more use of their time in the library when hours are limited. For instance, do they borrow more as a result of reduced access? One thing that was not measured was social impact on the community.

■ *Closures*: on average one-fifth of former library users did not use another library after their local library closed. For children the figure was generally much higher, with up to two-thirds of children in one area impacted by closures not able to find alternative provision. Adults questioned in the areas affected expressed great concern with this situation:

> Both parents and teachers believed that the impact of local library closure on young children was particularly severe. Their mention of the loss of a resource for general educational support, a resource for homework and an aid to literacy was not unexpected. However, what came out just as strongly was the way in which both parents and teachers felt the local library visit provided a much broader range of learning opportunities. The ability of a child to choose books for itself, to seek help from and talk to 'safe' adults, and to visit the library independently were all mentioned in the context of building self-confidence and social skills.
>
> (Proctor, Lee and Reilly, 1998, 83)

The 1998 report is the most recent large scale study to date of the issue of reduced opening hours and closures.

Conclusion

It is essential for the modern public library service to be as inclusive as possible. The concerns raised by the Muddiman et al. study (2000) force the profession to examine how accurate beliefs in the fundamental inclusiveness of libraries have been. As Train, Dalton and Elkin (2000) have suggested:

> The librarian should . . . reach out to the local communities, forging links and developing sustainable partnerships. In promoting a culture of inclusion, and at the same time celebrating the individuality of the library user, the librarian will maximise opportunities for all people. All library staff must be proud of the contribution they make to the inclusive society, and should learn to articulate this contribution to all.

The nature of true equity of access necessitates the public librarian having a thorough understanding of the needs of the community they serve, and ensuring through partnerships and networks that they are using all available options to enhance and deliver those services.

The ethical dimensions to equity should be the driver for all public librarians, as inherent in the codes of Ranganathan and Gorman is the belief that all human beings have a right to access the knowledge of their peers. Public libraries offer the best possible opportunity to achieve this through their services.

References

ALA (1995) *Code of Ethics of the American Library Association*, American Library Association,
www.ala.org/ala/oif/statementspols/codeofethics/codeethics.htm.

ALIA (2005) *Australian Library and Information Association: statement on professional conduct*,
www.alia.org.au/policies/professional.conduct.html.

Brandon, J. and Murray, D. (2007) *Hate on the State: how British libraries encourage Islamic extremism*, Centre for Social Cohesion,
www.socialcohesion.co.uk/pdf/HateOnTheState.pdf.

Cabinet Office (2008) *Context for Social Exclusion Work*,
www.cabinetoffice.gov.uk/social_exclusion_task_force/
context.aspx.

CILIP (2005) *Ethical Principles and Code of Professional Practice for Library and Information Professionals*, Chartered Institute of Library and Information Professionals, www.cilip.org.uk/policyadvocacy/ethics.

DCMS (1999) *Libraries for All: social inclusion in public libraries*, Department for Culture, Media and Sport.

Ezard, J. (1986) Library Ban for Murdoch Papers 'Snowballing', *Guardian*, 22 March, www.lexisnexis.com.

Gorman, M. (2000) *Our Enduring Values: librarianship in the 21st century*, American Library Association.

IFLA (2004) *IFLA/UNESCO Public Library Manifesto 1994*, www.ifla.org/VII/s8/unesco/eng.htm.

Muddiman, D., Durrani, S., Dutch, M., Linley, R., Pateman, J. and Vincent, J. (2000) *Open to All? The public library and social exclusion*, Resource.

Orton, G. I. J. (1980) *An Illustrated History of Mobile Library Services in the United Kingdom*, Branch and Mobile Libraries Group.

Proctor, R., Lee, H. and Reilly, R. (1998) *Access to Public Libraries: the impact of opening hours reductions and closures 1986-1997*, British Library Research and Innovation Centre.

Ranganathan, S. R. (1931) *The Five Laws of Library Science*, Madras Library Association.

Train, B., Dalton, P. and Elkin, J. (2000) Embracing Inclusion: the critical role of the library, *Library Management*, **21** (9), 483-90.

Usherwood, B. (2007) *Equity and Excellence in the Public Library: why ignorance is not our heritage*, Ashgate.

Vincent, J. (2007) *Welcome to Your Library: connecting public libraries and refugee communities*, Good Practice Guide, www.welcometoyourlibrary.org.uk/content_files/files/ WTYLGoodPracticeGuideNov07.pdf.

Wilson, K. and Birdi, B. (2008) *The Right 'Man' For The Job? The role of empathy in community librarianship*, University of Sheffield, Department of Information Studies.

Chapter 4

Cultural and leisure roles

Introduction

Public libraries offer vital cultural and leisure roles for the communities they serve. The provision of books, periodicals, music, films, documentaries and other resources opens up new worlds of culture and leisure to library members who are able to gain access to materials they may not necessarily otherwise be able to afford.

However, as discussed in previous chapters, it could be argued that public libraries in the UK were formed on the back of suspicions about the leisure pursuits of working class people; as Hayes and Morris have suggested, a 'strong argument for the establishment of public libraries related to the reform of leisure, recognizing them as a means of providing better recreational opportunities for working class people' (Hayes and Morris, 2005, 76). As will be seen in the discussion below, despite the genuinely positive notion of providing equity of access discussed in Chapter 3, public libraries can face criticism regarding the types of material they deliver to the public they serve.

This chapter will focus on the services provided by the public library that can be defined as supporting the cultural and leisure needs of the communities it serves, and consider some of the larger philosophical questions related to that provision.

Culture or leisure?

First, it is important to consider the philosophical context of libraries providing access to books. A fundamental debate about the existence of public libraries centres around the tension some commentators see between the public library supporting leisure reading and interests, versus its role to support the cultural needs of the community. In reality both are supported, but the pressure for libraries to be seen to be supporting usage that is worthy and educational rather than recreational has been with us since the formation of public libraries.

Lending of books – which kind?

This debate, dubbed the Great Fiction Question, relates to whether it is desirable for public funds to pay for people to read for leisure, or whether we should have more lofty ideals for our publicly funded libraries. The debate is constantly revisited both within the profession and without in wider society; one only has to recall the wish of the Select Committee cited in Chapter 2: 'Shall we therefore abandon the people to the influence of a low, enfeebling, and often pestilential literature, instead of enabling them to breathe a more elevated, and more congenial atmosphere?'(House of Commons, 1849, vii).

There is little doubt here that the framers of the original Act saw the public library as an access point for high quality reading material and not low brow fiction. This was a vision shared by many people working in libraries also. Long before and after the profession formed The Library Association in 1877, discussions have raged about the desirability of fiction lending within public libraries. As Snape highlights: 'The Great Fiction Question presented librarians with an insoluble dilemma. If libraries refused to buy fiction, or restricted fiction to novels of literary merit, their popular appeal would be immediately diminished and their rate of use would fall; furthermore librarians would be accused of assuming the mantle of public censor' (1995, 62).

Of course the debate, as Snape clearly points out, is not merely related to whether fiction should be lent or not, but also about the quality of the fiction lent. Libraries face an age-old dilemma of whether to promote library use through populist appeal, or to try to make available quality fiction in the hope that the aspiration of readers will draw them in that direction. Restricting access to what is deemed popular fiction could be seen as censorship by some, but equally in pursuing a populist agenda it would be possible for a library to simply stock its shelves with only best sellers, impacting on breadth of collection and restricting access to quality for those who want it.

Usherwood has recently passionately revisited this debate over the provision of quality and the potential clash with populism in his work *Equity and Excellence in the Public Library* (2007).

Ex Libris

The most high profile challenge on public libraries, certainly in the period since the 1980s, was the 1986 publication by the Adam Smith Institute entitled *Ex Libris*. Its main thesis was that public libraries were not a justifiable public expense because they served too narrow a portion of society, whose members could easily afford to pay for the leisure service they were enjoying. The report also argued that public libraries damaged the economic rights of publishers and authors due to the loss in sales revenue as a result of the ability to borrow the items. In the introduction the authors stated that 'Public libraries are perceived as desirable institutions by a largely uncritical man in the street. It is a position few other areas of the public sector enjoy – and one that is less easy to justify' (Adam Smith Institute, 1986, 4).

The suggestion was that public libraries were now a bloated network that too readily relied on public funding to provide what was a largely leisure role. It also challenged the legal requirements not to charge for the lending of books, when it was quite common to charge for other materials such as records, stating that it is 'difficult to see why borrowing a Mills and Boon romance should raise issues of principle very different from the borrowing of a recording of Beethoven or Bach' (41).

A key emphasis of the arguments in the report was that public libraries are used more by the middle classes than working classes, perhaps a dated notion based on the demographics of mid 1980s Britain rather than reflective of any modern reality; this led to the argument that 'Those who benefit from libraries are those who use them, whether as individuals seeking relaxing reading or commercial interests seeking profits. It seems only right that they should pay for the benefits they receive rather than be subsidized by the rest of society or, indeed, by those whose works they borrow rather than buy' (53).

Certainly *Ex Libris* reflected a viewpoint that the only measure of benefit that could be accrued from the lending of books was economic, and rather than aiding the economy, public libraries were actually damaging it by destroying any competition in the provision of lending materials and by limiting the income of authors and publishers.

The report was released to much public and professional comment due to its controversial stance on the free public library service, but it raised fundamental points for public libraries to consider in terms of who was accessing services and who was not.

Public lending right

Public lending right (PLR), touched on as a major issue within *Ex Libris*, is based on the notion that authors of books deserve a financial reward when public libraries lend copies of their works.

The PLR movement began to gain prominence in the UK in the 1970s based on other European models that had existed for some time whereby authors were recompensed for the works written by them and borrowed through libraries. The 1979 Public Lending Right Act enshrined PLR in UK law and the subsequent PLR office was set up to administer the programme that resulted once the PLR scheme had been agreed by Parliament in 1982.

Any author who wishes to make a claim under PLR must register with the PLR office; the maximum that could be allocated in 2008 to an author was £6600, based on a rate of 6 pence per loan.

Borrowing of books in practice

Notwithstanding the debates highlighted above, the most commonly known function of the public library remains the lending of books to its members. It is in this free exchange of culture and knowledge that the public library could be seen to be serving its most vital function: putting books and other materials in the hands of those who cannot afford them.

To maintain a competent system of lending books the public library needs an infrastructure to support the acquisition, processing and delivering of stock to library users. The most vital goal of that infrastructure is to ensure efficiency of circulation of materials. Circulation control encompasses the processes created to ensure that stock is ordered, processed and made available for lending to library users.

Stock selection

Traditionally the selection of stock for public libraries has been a professional task undertaken by librarians. How this was done varied from library authority to library authority. In some cases the librarian in charge of a specific branch library would have the key role in selecting materials for their library. In others the responsibility would be team driven, and a group of librarians would undertake the stock selection for an entire library system, ensuring that the service had enough copies of titles to satisfy demand. Sometimes a mixture of the two methods would be used, with branch libraries allowed to choose from a collection of new items that had been preselected by a team.

A crucial document to enable library services to communicate their stock selection criteria to their users is a stock development policy. This is normally a document, made available via the website of the local library, or in such a way as to enable library users to access it and understand what criteria the library uses to develop stock. A good example of a stock development policy is provided by Rotherham Library Service; their document clearly states information on:

- aims and objectives of the policy: what it is trying to achieve and how it helps the better management of the service
- budget allocation: how budget decisions related to the book fund are made
- stock selection for children and young people: the nature of the stock for different age groups
- stock selection for adults: meeting needs of users and non-users
- stock selection for non-fiction and non-book materials: specific criteria, such as health and well-being

- local materials: how the library service will support the building of collections on the local area
- donations: potentially a contentious issue for libraries, therefore how they are dealt with and whether they are welcome
- reservations and requests: how reservations are dealt with, and what are the waiting periods and borrowing periods when material has been requested
- procurement and processing: how books are selected and how long it takes until they are available for users from order.

(Rotherham Library and Information Service, 2004)

Individual librarians often have the task of ensuring stock is purchased for a specific user group. The notion behind this is that the librarian can become a subject expert in that area and thus ensure that the library's holdings are comprehensive and meet the needs of that group. Examples include children's and young people's librarians and librarians responsible for purchasing materials for particular ethnic groups.

Larger reference libraries may also have librarians charged with purchasing materials in specific subject areas. In each of these cases the librarian builds up an expertise in their area of interest and can efficiently select materials appropriate for the user group or subject matter they are responsible for. These are tasks that involve building not only a subject knowledge but also the ability to be a good networker and to work with all the relevant community groups necessary to ensure provision meets the needs of the group.

Supplier selection

A new approach to selection of materials for public libraries that has become popular in recent years is that of supplier selection. This is a route that has government backing through the MLA report, *Better Stock, Better Libraries* (MLA, 2006).

The report advocated increased use of the private sector in the stock procurement process, citing several case studies where efficiencies had been gained by passing more of the work to suppliers rather than librarians. One of the case studies cited in the consultant's report was that of the

London Libraries Consortium, of which both Tower Hamlets and Waltham Forest, two of the library authorities discussed in the *Hate on the State* report, are members. The MLA report suggested that it was the intention within the consortium 'to move to supplier selection as far as possible' (MLA, 2006, 47).

Promotion of literacy and reading

One of the major goals of the public library is to encourage reading among members and in wider society. Indeed, this is one of the reasons forward thinking individuals developed the concept of a free and unrestricted public library service in the 19th century. As Train suggests, 'Proponents of the public library service believe that reading has an intrinsic value to all citizens, not only in a formal educational setting, but as a means of informing and enhancing the lives of all who choose to use it' (Train, 2003, 30).

As will be seen later in the chapter a lot of the emphasis in this area is related to the promotion of reading to children and young people; however, the role of the library in the literacy of the adult population cannot be underestimated. The promotion of reading in and of itself is a positive goal, and other recent initiatives have helped to enhance this and develop the reading interests of library users of all ages.

Reader development

Reading promotion can take a variety of forms. It can encompass something as straightforward as presenting a themed display of books, perhaps on one author or subject, or on a geographical theme. Reading can also be promoted through a national programme aimed at reaching as much of the population as possible, perhaps a television book club, or such like. At the root of such initiatives is the desire to promote reading to users, and in some cases to expand their reading into unfamiliar areas. Intervention in the reading habits of library users has been defined as reader development (Train, 2003). The concept of reader development has been further defined as 'a body of professional practice which encouraged readers to open up their reading choices, share their reading experiences and raise the status of reading as a creative activity' (CILIP, 2007).

Reader development differs from traditional reading promotion in a key way, however, as rather than being focused on the collection, the author or the subject, the emphasis is on the reader. While an eventual goal could be perceived as being encouraging readers to read better, the crucial component is to encourage them to read wider and differently. This is an important distinction, since the core of reader development is not about elitism in literature, but about truly engaging the reader with the reading process and enhancing their enjoyment of different kinds of books.

The Branching Out initiative ran from 1998–2006 and promoted good practice in reader development, with an emphasis on training of staff to understand how reader development is undertaken in libraries. They defined reader development as follows: 'Reader development sells the reading experience and what it can do for you, rather than selling individual books or writers. It builds the audience for literature by moving readers beyond brand loyalty to individual writers, helping them develop the confidence to try something new' (Opening the Book, 2008a).

A key deliverable of the project was the development of an online course, Frontline, which consisted of seven modules focused on:

- readers
- library staff
- reader-to-reader
- books and audiences
- displaying books
- targeting a promotion
- running a promotion.   (Opening the Book, 2008b)

The number of resources and aid for library staff wishing to expand reader development initiatives has grown significantly in the past ten years. As part of its National Reading Campaign, the Literacy Trust hosts a web page offering links to further information and ideas related to reader development (Literacy Trust, 2008). The growth in reader development initiatives has also mirrored the growth in reading groups, and websites containing reader reviews of books and advice on books to read.

A useful project funded by the Big Lottery Fund and produced by Opening the Book created a website, Whichbook.net, which allows readers to use a set of scales on themes to select reading materials (Opening the Book, 2008c). Users of the site click on a scale and drag the slider to the theme they wish to have recommendations on. Themes reflect potential moods, therefore they include scales such as happy to sad, funny to serious, gentle to violent, sex to no sex, conventional to unusual, and short to long. Once recommendations fitting the criteria are found the user can click a link that eventually allows them to check their local library catalogue to ascertain if the book is available.

Reading groups

Reading groups are increasingly popular both in and independently of public libraries. Clearly libraries are well placed to offer such an activity, since they have the venue and the stock available for potential members to consult.

Differing models for reading groups in libraries exist. Some take the form of staff-led discussions, where the group selects material for reading, but the discussions themselves are facilitated by the library staff member. Other models do not involve the library staff at all, with the library being used as a venue and supplier of reading materials only.

In research undertaken on reading groups, Scothern (2000) found that leadership in the group and having a good mix of people from different backgrounds and interests were crucial in group success. She also found that reading groups in libraries enhanced the library in ways other than the group having a presence, and they worked as excellent marketing opportunities for library outreach.

The Reading Agency

The Reading Agency (www.readingagency.org.uk) is a national charity that is at the heart of many of the most innovative reader development programmes in the UK. Using partners from broadcasting and commercial areas, it encourages the growth of reading using quality marketing materials themed around specific initiatives.

Partnerships with broadcasters include several initiatives with the BBC, as well as promoting Channel 4's Richard & Judy Book Club within public libraries, and the ITV Crime Thriller Awards. A key role of the Agency is to connect public libraries with such national programmes, and encouraging the use of public libraries to engage with them. Rather than buy the books necessary to take part in the Richard & Judy Book Club, for instance, the viewer can instead visit the local library and borrow them.

The Agency also undertakes several high profile programmes for children and young people, which will be discussed in more detail below.

Bibliotherapy

Studies suggest that reading can also have a beneficial impact on the health of the reader. The concept of bibliotherapy can be approached from a range of professional viewpoints, from those in the health field to those in book promotion, but a shared view for all is the belief that the book can have a transformational benefit on the person reading it.

In recent research, however, Brewster (2007) discovered that people have a range of interpretations of what bibliotherapy is within public library services, including everything from 'informal bibliotherapy' to clinical programmes aimed at users with mental health issues and involving the input of local doctors.

Children and young people's services

Librarians dealing with children and young people are some of the most vital professionals in the library and information profession. As important to the development of a child as a good teacher, an enthusiastic, passionate and knowledgeable children's librarian can open up a child's world view by showing them the wonders of reading that are contained in the library collections.

However, the children's librarian not only promotes the love of the book to the child; a crucial component in their work is to impart library research skills by instructing children in the use of the library's collections. Indeed the role of the children's librarian is nothing less than helping to introduce the child to the world of books, information and reading.

Services for babies and toddlers

The promotion of reading to children starts at a very young age. Through the excellent work of the Bookstart scheme (www.bookstart.co.uk) every child born in the UK is given a pack containing two board books, with a booklet for the parent discussing the importance of reading to their child. Parents are also given a library card for their child and encouraged to visit the library to engage with other library activities for babies and toddlers.

One such activity under the auspices of Bookstart is a bounce and tickle session. These involve parents taking their child to organized sessions where they are led in singing nursery rhymes to their child while following the actions of the leader. These sessions have been found to be immensely enjoyable for both parent and child, and the nursery rhymes used are traditional favourites that have stood the test of time.

Summer Reading Challenge

An initiative of The Reading Agency and in its tenth year in 2008, the Summer Reading Challenge offers the opportunity for children to engage in a reading challenge while on their summer holidays from school.

The 2008 campaign theme was tied in with the Beijing Olympics and thus had an emphasis on books about sport. Entitled Team Read, it encouraged children to read six books over their summer holiday break, and they earned a bronze, silver or gold medal level depending on how many they read. Events on the theme were also held in many libraries, using branded material from The Reading Agency bearing the Team Read logos.

Chatterbooks

Another Reading Agency initiative that takes place throughout the year is the Chatterbooks programme. Sponsored by the telecom company Orange, the goal is to encourage children aged between 4 and 12 to become confident about talking about the books they read. They visit the library with their family and join a Chatterbooks group, where they can share their views on the books with other children.

Their Reading Futures

The Reading Agency also operates the site Their Reading Futures (www.theirreadingfutures.org.uk) aimed at professional librarians and teachers bringing together resources and information for anyone involved in encouraging children and young people to read. The site also contains e-learning packages for professionals who wish to improve their skills in promoting reading to young people.

Requirements for quality children's services

Children and Young People: Library Association Guidelines for Public Library Services set out the requirements for a quality service for young people (Blanshard, 1997). The guidelines emphasize that this work is so important that there should be at least two specialist children's librarian posts within a library authority. More specifically the guidelines recommend that there should be a senior specialist children's post that is part of the senior management team of a public library service.

The guidelines stress the importance of training staff, not only those involved with working directly with young people's programmes, but other staff who are not charged with this remit (Blanshard, 1997, 42-3).

The *Start with the Child* report produced in 2002 also highlighted strands that should be present when attempting to provide services for young people:

■ *appropriate environments and services*: safe and welcoming environments that children want to spend time in
■ *services that are relevant and responsive*: up to date materials of interest to the user group, to be available in a timely and efficient manner
■ *appropriate help for children and young people and for those who support them*: aid in using services, with specialist staff on hand to provide programmes of interest
■ *support from the community at large to use and benefit from services*: promotion of the library service within the community and help to access the services if necessary.

(CILIP, 2002, 11)

The report suggested that children and young people needed encouragement to use the library and services geared towards their interests and needs.

Carnegie and Greenaway awards

Children's librarians also have a major role in the promotion of two of the key book awards in children's publishing. Both are sponsored by CILIP. The Carnegie Award is for the best children's book of the year, and the Greenaway Award is for distinguished illustration in a children's book. The shortlists for both are selected by a panel made up of representatives from the different regional branches of the Youth Libraries Group (YLG), the special interest group of CILIP related to children's librarianship. The final award is voted on by a panel of 12 judges drawn from the membership of YLG.

Through the selection and award of both medals, the children's librarians of the UK cement their role at the heart of children's book publishing and promotion in the UK.

Music, films and other media

Technology has for a long time enabled people to listen to music or watch films or other visual productions in their own homes. It has thus been a logical extension for public libraries to offer access to such cultural materials for their members.

The main cultural argument for public libraries offering access to such media relates to the breadth of choice that can become available to library users. Rather than providing a narrow range of popular materials such as blockbuster movies or the top 20 albums, public libraries can make available a range of different types of media, including those specializing in classical music and world and independent cinema.

Libraries have had audio collections for many decades, which library users can try, perhaps sampling different types of music, possibly before deciding to purchase an item. More recently the same provision has been made for lending films on DVD.

Lending of such materials brings in an income, which is lucrative, since audiovisual materials can be charged for. The issues surrounding this will be discussed in more detail in Chapter 8.

Conclusion

It is unlikely that the debate around public libraries providing access to reading materials of questionable quality will ever go away. It remains a core concern, and is often a stick to beat the service with.

Librarians must be aware of the pros and cons of the Great Fiction Question. Calls to ensure value for money in library services can lead to the unwelcome goal of trying to maximize book issues and lead to a culture of libraries buying only what is popular and what will be issued many times. On the surface this may suggest a success of sorts, but if the role of the library and staff to promote reading and widen the horizons of readers is in any way undermined or diminished, the library becomes little more than a storehouse rather than a proactive community facility.

Promoting reading and encouraging more people to borrow from the public library is an intrinsically positive aim for librarians. Using the innovative techniques of reader development librarians can help readers branch out into new types of reading material. Those holding the posts should challenge themselves intellectually and culturally by exposing themselves to new ideas and viewpoints. National programmes such as those promoted by The Reading Agency help libraries in the UK to communicate a cohesive message to borrowers through high quality marketing and promotion.

This can be difficult in an environment where libraries are encouraged to emphasize the importance of issue figures and thus buy what is popular to satisfy stated needs. The reading interests of users cannot be developed and widened overnight, and it is only possible to promote new ways of reading if staff are allowed time to engage with individuals and produce high quality materials to aid them in their reading habits.

Wider cultural interest in reading is reflected in such television programmes as *Richard & Judy*, and although such initiatives are not necessarily library driven, there is little doubt that they encourage people to read and bring people into public libraries to gain access to the books recommended on the programme.

Finally, the importance of the work undertaken by librarians working with children and young people cannot be underestimated. Their role in promoting a love of books and reading to the adults of the future is crucial for society, and their special knowledge of the world of children's publishing needs to be consistently recognized and applauded by the profession at large and society in general. If services of this nature are scaled down, not only is quality of service reduced, but such decisions also reflect a lack of belief in our own aspirations for the potential of our young people.

References

Adam Smith Institute (1986) *Ex Libris*, ASI (Research) Ltd.

Blanshard, C. (ed.) (1997) *Children and Young People: Library Association Guidelines for Public Library Services*, 2nd edn, Library Association.

Brewster, E. (2007) *'Medicine for the Soul': bibliotherapy and the public library*, unpublished MA thesis, University of Sheffield, http://dagda.shef.ac.uk/dissertations/2006-07/External/ Brewster_Elizabeth_MALib.pdf.

CILIP (2002) *Start with the Child: report of the CILIP working group on library provision for children and young people*, CILIP, www.cilip.org.uk/specialinterestgroups/bysubject/youth/ publications/youngpeople/startwiththechild/.

CILIP (2007) *Reader Development*, www.cilip.org.uk/informationadvice/readerdevelopment/.

Hayes, E. and Morris, A. (2005) Leisure Roles of Public Libraries, *Journal of Librarianship and Information Science*, **37** (3), 131-9.

House of Commons (1849) *Report of the Select Committee on Public Libraries Together with the Minutes of Evidence and Appendix*, House of Commons.

Literacy Trust (2008) *Resources for Libraries and Reader Development*, www.literacytrust.org.uk/Database/libraryres.html.

MLA (2006) *Better Stock, Better Libraries: transforming library stock procurement*, Museums, Libraries and Archives Council, www.mla.gov.uk/resources/assets//B/better_stock_better_ libraries_10123.pdf.

Opening the Book (2008a) *Branching Out: archive*, www.openingthebook.com/archive/branching-out/.

Opening the Book (2008b) *Frontline Demonstration*, www.openingthebook.co.uk/frontline/demo/.

Opening the Book (2008c) *Whichbook.net*,
    www.whichbook.net.
Rotherham Library and Information Service (2004) *Stock Management Policy*, 3rd edn,
    www.rotherham.gov.uk/NR/rdonlyres/1BBB2873-BB6C-4860-8771-9922719EEBC3/0/Stock_Policy_2004.pdf.
Scothern, C. (2000) *What Makes a Successful Public Library Reading Group? How good practice can be created and sustained*, unpublished MA thesis, University of Sheffield,
    http://dagda.shef.ac.uk/dissertations/1999-00/scothern.pdf.
Snape, R. (1995) *Leisure and the Rise of the Public Library*, Library Association Publishing.
Train, B. (2003) Reader Development. In Elkin, J., Train, B. and Denham, D., *Reading and Reader Development: the pleasure of reading*, Facet Publishing.
Usherwood, B. (2007) *Equity and Excellence in the Public Library: why ignorance is not our heritage*, Ashgate.

Chapter 5

Information, advice and informed citizenship

Introduction

The public library has a vital role to play as a source of trusted and impartial information within its community and in society. As discussed in Chapter 2, this role is historical and the library staff serve as the intermediaries for the user.

We all need information to go about our daily lives successfully. Yet the information needs of an entire community are potentially complex, and library users require information at different levels. Some need simple forms of information, others need more complex forms. The types of information we may need are diverse, everything from a bus or train timetable, to leaflets on benefits, legal rights, health issues and careers. This is in addition to the more common reference enquiries that libraries regularly undertake, for example checking facts in encyclopedias or directories, or telephone numbers for companies or other organizations. Public libraries provide access to these and other types of information for their communities.

Information sources selected for users need to be authoritative and accurate, and library staff need to be able to find the correct information for their users as quickly and efficiently as possible.

This chapter will discuss:

- the types of information public libraries regularly provide for users
- the ethical and service challenges in delivering information to users
- the reference interview
- the range of services provided by public libraries that can be broadly defined as information services.

Information types

Staff in public libraries must be prepared for enquiries of all types and therefore provide a range of resources, such as:

- commercially produced reference books, encyclopedias and the like
- information on the local authority and other governmental sources
- information on the local history of their area
- community information
- information on genealogy and family history.

In addition some public libraries offer even more specialist types of reference information, for example on careers, businesses or even health via professionals qualified in the area.

Specialist reference materials can be an expensive resource for libraries. This high cost is not only related to the limited market for the books, but is also the result of the amount of work that goes into producing many specialist reference works. A reference work loses its usefulness if it is out of date, thus many of the more staple resources for libraries are published annually. Increasingly as ICT has become more prevalent in libraries many reference works are accessed via electronic means, increasingly through the internet.

This has pros and cons for the library and user. The information in reference works that are available on the internet can be updated much more frequently than in the printed version, which is normally several months out of date when published. Making reference works available on the internet also allows more than one user to consult the same resource at any time. Public libraries are increasingly allowing users to access reference resources from outside the library; subscriptions to electronic services often come with licences that allow library members to access them even from their own homes. Often the barcode number of the member's library card is used as identification for logging in to such databases.

The downside to providing access to reference works via the internet relates to what the library is actually buying. If the purchase does not include a physical copy that the library can store alongside the electronic product, then essentially the library is buying access to a database rather than a physical item. This means that the library will no longer have an archive of that particular work and can only continue to provide access if it pays the appropriate fee. If for any reason the library can no longer, or chooses not to, sustain the subscription fee then it may also lose its archive of the publication.

Thus the increasing use of electronic reference materials poses challenges to traditional library acquisition and collection development models that need to be understood and grappled with.

Ethics of information – any question answered?

A fundamental ethical question with which the library profession continually grapples is whether there are any questions that public library staff cannot or should not answer?

If public libraries aim to provide access to all sorts of information there are likely to be occasions when the nature of the information being sought raises some eyebrows. A researcher on ethics in librarianship, Robert Hauptman, conducted such an experiment in 1975 when he visited 13 libraries in California, six public and seven academic, and requested from the reference librarian information on how much cordite it would take to create a bomb capable of destroying a small suburban home (Hauptman, 1976). To their credit, or discredit depending on your viewpoint, all 13 libraries provided the information requested.

In a more recent experiment in ethics carried out in Slovenia, students from a library school asked several public libraries for access to information on committing suicide and necrophilia, and for images of corpses (Juznic et al., 2001). Their findings suggested that the information was provided to the limits of the librarians' willingness to search; in other words the issue was not what the librarian was willing to provide from an ethical standpoint, but how good they were at finding information and the quality of resources at their disposal.

All of this raises a key dilemma for public librarians: what kinds of information should be provided from a publicly funded institution? As there is a significant chance that most information queries are now handled by paraprofessional staff who are very likely to have no training or background in ethics, there is a further dimension to the issue. If such staff are not members of an appropriate professional body such as CILIP they may have no means of knowing what the ethical challenges for the library and information profession are and what their responsibilities are to the user, the organization and wider society in dealing with them. Readers of this book who are interested in stipulated ethical responsibilities for their members from a range of library associations might like to consult *A Handbook of Ethical Practice* (McMenemy, Poulter and Burton, 2006) which provides an overview and comparison of a range of ethical codes from different parts of the library world. The code for Members of CILIP is discussed in more detail in Chapter 10.

It could be argued that if a piece of information is legal and accessible then it should be provided, but this in itself raises fundamental challenges of ethical and legal significance. For instance, recent legislation passed to counter terrorism in the UK raises major challenges for librarians. The Terrorism Act 2006 makes it illegal to be reckless in providing someone with information that could later be used in a terrorist activity. This is not an issue of minor importance for a librarian; it has great potential to place the library in a situation whereby it is breaking the law by providing access to collections it holds.

Thus the librarian has to balance the right of the user to access a piece of information against the best interest of society in providing it, notwithstanding the legal issues involved.

Reference services

Reference services are vital to any public library service. Often users are not interested in borrowing any particular book but want the answer to a question or simple information, without any awareness of which library resource will provide it. This is where the librarian's specialized knowledge of the library collections and appropriate reference sources comes into play. As Denis Grogan has argued:

> It is a serious error to think that reference work is simply a matter of answering questions. Experienced librarians can quote many examples of questions taken at their face value and answered in a perfectly adequate manner, but which still left the reader far from satisfied. It is far better thought of as problem-solving, with the actual identification of the reader's problem being just as important as hunting for the information.
>
> (Grogan, 1987, 37)

There are three broad types of reference enquiries regularly faced by librarians in all types of library (Grogan, 1992):

- *Administrative and directional enquiries*: responding to these queries requires a general knowledge of the library building and facilities available to the user. These queries are normally related to questions regarding library policies, equipment information and other such broadly administrative tasks. For example, a user might seek help in using the library photocopier, a microfilm machine or the like. Or someone might ask about the library's borrowing rules or have other administrative queries about joining the library.
- *Author/title enquiries*: public librarians who answer bibliographical enquiries often need specialist knowledge. Although the library catalogue can answer many of them, a large number of such queries relate to journal articles. Efficient reference librarians are knowledgeable about the abstracting and indexing tools available in the library to steer people towards ways of finding similar or linked articles. Library users often do not know about such tools, which offer an excellent way of enhancing a user's depth of searching on a topic. More specialized indexing and abstracting tools are not available in the majority of public libraries, so sometimes librarians seek the aid of a larger library, perhaps the central reference library in the local authority, or a larger regional library that has an extensive collection

of such resources. Users often do not know the exact title of the item they are looking for, but use a common title. Grogan (1987) cites the Universal Declaration of Human Rights and the Aquarian Gospel as examples of this; enquiries about items using their common title are called known-item or verification enquiries. In these cases the user and the librarian are pretty sure that the user is asking for something that exists, but need to find its true title in order to access it. Librarians working in the mid to late 1990s will likely remember a common enquiry of this type that followed the use of a W. H. Auden poem in the film *Four Weddings and a Funeral*. Frequently librarians were asked for a copy of 'Stop all the clocks', when the actual title of the poem was 'Funeral Blues'. Grogan differentiates these types of queries from their opposite, not-known item or identification queries (Grogan, 1992, 37-8).

■ *Fact-finding enquiries*: these are commonly known as quick reference or ready reference queries. They might be questions requiring a simple answer, such as 'Who was prime minister in 1950?', or other factual questions. In responding to fact-finding queries librarians need not only a thorough knowledge of the available stock, but also a good sense of general knowledge to enable them to understand the nature and context of the query. The meat of the query is normally drawn out of the user by a process known as the reference interview.

Reference interviews

The process known as the reference interview is a regular interaction in libraries of all kinds, where the librarian attempts to respond to a user query by providing the most accurate information possible. This is not necessarily just a case of responding directly to a posed question with an answer, although for many users this will suffice. More often than not it is a process of teasing from the user what exactly their need is and then finding the correct resource to satisfy that need; importantly the competent librarian must always be aware that stated want does not always equate to actual need. There are three crucial points that the librarian must consider:

- that there is no misunderstanding over the meaning of the question posed
- that the question accurately represents what the library user wants
- that what the reader wants will satisfy their problem or need.

(Grogan, 1987, 37-8)

Many library users are independent searchers and visit the reference section of the library and browse without seeking input from the library staff. Such users may not require the librarian's aid in finding out information, but the librarian should always be accessible and willing to aid such users without appearing pushy or intrusive. Some library users may not know which resource is best able to satisfy their query, and a simple enquiry from the librarian as to the user's satisfaction with what they have found may be enough to allow a reference interview to take place and for the user to ensure they have used the library collections to the best effect.

Of crucial consideration is the increasing use by library users of internet search engines and other basic tools for information seeking. Without the appropriate intermediary to aid the search, it is debatable how efficient many users find such services if they do not articulate their need adequately. The library should provide adequate guides on search engine use near or on the computers to aid users in successfully navigating the internet. Library staff have a crucial role in training users to be competent and information-literate internet searchers. The responsibilities of the public library in the role of information literacy will be discussed in more detail later in the chapter.

Virtual reference services

The term virtual reference services describes services provided to library users who are in another location from the librarian when the query is presented. In recent times the term is used mainly for internet-based services such as instant messaging and e-mail.

Service challenges

The challenges inherent in providing a good quality virtual reference service are similar to those faced in providing a reference service in the analogue world, but there are many others. Although the same concerns with the quality of the reference interview are relevant, it is far more difficult to ascertain without any physical cues whether a user understands what a librarian is saying, and whether the librarian correctly understands the user. Kovacs (2007) has provided a helpful guide for librarians undertaking virtual reference services with advice on the technologies, and how to interact with the user in this new world.

Virtual reference services can be either synchronous or asynchronous. For a service to be synchronous it has to be a real-time interaction with the library user, normally through some kind of instant messaging client running on the computers of the librarian and the user. Asynchronous virtual reference is where the interaction is not undertaken in real time, such as an e-mail exchange back and forward, which necessitates waiting for the other party to reply.

People's Network – Enquire

In the UK an initiative introduced as part of the ongoing People's Network programme (www.peoplesnetwork.gov.uk/) has built on work previously undertaken in the late 1990s through the Ask a Librarian service, into a service called Enquire.

The Enquire service is run collaboratively between 80 public library services throughout England and Scotland, whose staff take turns in providing a virtual reference service for users, accessible via the link above. Users complete a small form stating their name, e-mail address and question, although the interaction can be anonymous. The transcript of the interaction with the librarian is saved and can be e-mailed to the user or a link is made available which the user can click on in order to receive the transcript anonymously. The service is available during office hours during the week, but outside these hours an agreement with American library services allows users to gain access to an American librarian to answer questions.

Guidelines for reference and information services

In 1999 the Information Services Group (ISG) produced a set of guidelines for public libraries related to reference and information services. The ISG is the special interest group of CILIP that focuses on information services.

The guidelines focus on all aspects of the reference service within a public library, including:

- users
- the information service
- information resources
- ICT
- accommodation
- management
- quality of service and performance measurement
- publicity and promotion.   (Information Services Group, 1999)

They set out clearly what library services of differing sizes should include as a part of their collections, recognizing that not all libraries need to have exactly the same provision, and that larger reference libraries will inevitably have more specialist reference materials than a community library. Crucially it also states what the requirements for a small community library should be in terms of reference materials.

The International Federation of Library Associations (IFLA) Reference and Information Services Section has also created a set of guidelines for libraries delivering digital reference services (IFLA, 2006).

Informed citizenship

Public libraries have a major role to play in helping build an informed citizenship. The notion of the informed citizen is that each individual has access to the most appropriate, up to date and accurate information they need to go about their daily lives as citizens. For public libraries aiding informed citizenship is about providing access to content and imparting skills in best use of information to users. It is not enough for the library to offer access to the materials users need; they need easy pathways into that material through the use of high quality catalogues and indexes, and well trained staff to aid them in understanding and using it.

Information literacy

As well as providing access to materials, public libraries are responsible for ensuring that library users develop their skills in finding and using materials. Library instruction is as old as libraries themselves, whereby library staff help users identify and use the materials available, and instruct them how to evaluate and recognize high quality information sources.

Information literacy has been a major concern in academic librarianship for several years, so much so that the Standing Conference on National and University Libraries (SCONUL) has developed its *Seven Pillars of Information Literacy* (SCONUL, 2007) to formalize the concept. No such consideration has yet been given within the public library sector, however, and to date SCONUL's model remains the best to follow if considering information literacy in the public library context.

Advice

Public library staff cannot always offer advice to patrons, as the nature of offering advice necessitates the adviser having a specialism in the subject area. For instance library staff should not offer legal advice or advice on health unless they are qualified to do so. Leaving aside for a moment their provision of access to high quality books and information, public libraries are more useful as venues for advice to be offered by appropriate qualified professionals, rather than by library staff.

A positive way in which public libraries can offer health advice is illustrated via an initiative currently undertaken by East Renfrewshire Council in Scotland. The My Health programme (www.eastrenfrewshire. gov.uk/myhealth) offers a portal for accessing quality health information, including an e-learning module in health information, which can be undertaken to test knowledge. The portal also provides access to information on local health services and how to access them.

Government information and e-government

An important aspect of electronic government (e-government) is to provide access to elected officials and administrators. In the UK there was a government target that where possible public services should make their services internet-enabled by the end of 2005. This has largely been done and has enhanced access to e-commerce facilities on government websites, allowing services like car tax, council tax and income tax to be paid online.

E-government also encompasses access to elected officials, and it is straightforward to find the name of an elected official and an e-mail address on most e-government sites. E-government also allows citizens to access government policy documents and consultations. Public libraries have an important role for citizens in facilitating access to democratic life. For users without access to ICTs such access is problematic if not impossible.

Community information

There is no organization in the country better placed to gather and disseminate accurate information on local communities than the public library. Community libraries have gathered such information for decades and made it accessible to the local community.

Commercial organizations using geographic information systems have raised the bar in many ways in the provision of large bodies of community information. For instance many websites now offer the ability to enter a postcode and then to be presented with a great deal of information on the local area, such as businesses, schools, driving directions and house prices. Although it is difficult for public libraries in isolation to compete with such sophisticated systems, many systems that provide this sort of information do so for commercial reasons, such as offering easier findability to paid advertisers, and public libraries have an advantage over them by being impartial.

Business information

Many large businesses employ librarians or information managers to work for them, and they provide an immensely valuable service in gathering market data and information on competitors, as well as aiding in research and development, and archiving any available information on the company itself.

Most small to medium enterprises (SMEs) do not have the resources to hire staff for these functions, and public libraries can provide them with a crucial service by giving them access to information to aid their business interests.

In a study of business information provision in Yorkshire, Wilson and Train found that in the period of their observational study the majority of queries to the business information services they were evaluating were related to either market research or business start-up, suggesting that the business information services in question were offering a significant contribution to enterprise within the community (Wilson and Train, 2005, 42).

A useful example of a collaborative business information service offered by public libraries is the Ask About Business initiative (www. askaboutbusiness.org/site/), which is a collaborative partnership between 11 public library services in Greater Manchester. The initiative offers a service to companies within the area and combines the skills of all the libraries in delivering a high quality service.

Heritage and digitization services

Public libraries have historically stored material on their local areas, as well as other special collections that they may acquire through donation, bequest or purchase. It is not uncommon for such collections to have importance and interest outwith the geographic area covered by the library, for instance materials on local authors or prominent local families, or historical incidents. Accessing such materials can be problematic, as they are invariably unique collections and thus if there is continued use of them there is a risk that materials will be damaged through human contact and general wear and tear. Digitization offers libraries the ability to create digital versions of the collections and make them more readily available to local users and more widely through the internet.

A massive growth in digitization projects in public libraries occurred in the early part of the 21st century. Although many started with individual public libraries undertaking projects, there was also massive investment nationally from the New Opportunities Fund (NOF) under the People's Network programme.

It is apt that the focus on infrastructure and on content creation were seen as equally important, as the network that was built needed content that was of interest to the population who would be using the new computer terminals. The aim of the NOF-Digitise programme was 'to create innovative online resources of benefit to every UK citizen, bringing together over 500 partner organisations to create support for lifelong learning under the broad themes of citizenship, re-skilling, and cultural enrichment' (Nicholson and MacGregor, 2003, 96).

The £50 million investment led to the creation of a portal where users can access all projects funded under the initiative, Enrich UK, which is now part of the wider European Union project MICHAEL (Multilingual Inventory of Cultural Heritage in Europe).

Genealogy services

Genealogical research is one of the most popular pastimes on the internet; the popularity is evidenced by TV shows like *Who Do You Think You Are?*, which regularly gain millions of viewers and have accompanying computer programs and books to aid viewers in researching their own family history.

Supporting this kind of research has always been an important service for many public libraries throughout the UK. Although many of the more popular materials that used to be consulted in libraries such as census returns have been digitized, libraries continue to store other records unique to their own areas. For instance over the years some of the larger public libraries have acquired parish registers from local churches, crucial resources for family historians seeking to find out information that pre-dates the first UK census and before official national registers of births, deaths and marriages were recorded. Other resources might include old maps of the area that show houses and dwellings and even streets that no longer exist, as well as information and records on prominent local families.

Genealogical services also offer opportunities for revenue raising for the public library, which would otherwise be unable to devote staff time and expertise in satisfying such queries. Often such queries come from people who live outside the area, commonly abroad, so some library services feel it is reasonable to charge for providing services that are time consuming. Family historians are often used to having to pay for access to such materials, and certainly it has become an extremely lucrative commercial opportunity for some of the online providers.

Crucially the operation of efficient genealogical services necessitates knowledgeable and well trained staff who can inform users not only about the materials stored within the library itself, but also about genealogical resources held in other libraries. They should also be able to proffer advice on how to go about the process of researching family history. Although the general public is certainly better informed than it used to be about how time consuming an endeavour such research is, TV programmes can give a misleading impression of how easy it is to find this sort of information.

Information after civil disasters

Public libraries can have a key role within communities after major civic disasters or accidents have occurred. In a 1993 book Simmons discusses some examples of civic disasters where the local public library became a focal point for disseminating information to the local community. Often when a disaster happens getting information to people is a difficult endeavour, and thus having a trusted location as a central information resource for people is a huge advantage. Simmons (1993) gave examples of public libraries responding after disasters such as floods, the Hungerford massacre, and the Zeebrugge and Lockerbie disasters. Thus public libraries can act as a crucial community resource in a challenging time, offering a one-stop facility for access to crucial information on a developing situation.

Web services

Finally the importance of the web presence of a public library is a crucial consideration in the modern era. The library website serves two distinct functions:

- as an advert for the library and the service it operates
- as a gateway to information provided by the library.

Some of the services discussed earlier in the chapter such as web-based databases and virtual reference services should be made accessible via the library website. The library catalogue should also be accessible via the library website, enabling users to find out if the library stocks items they are interested in, to access their borrower record and to renew and reserve items.

The library website also offers the opportunity for the librarian to design high quality gateways into information for the library user. Links can be put together offering access to many of the subjects discussed earlier in the chapter, such as genealogy, business and health information. The website can become a trusted virtual gateway just as the library itself is a trusted physical source.

However, producing a high quality site can be a challenge for UK public libraries, as few have ownership of their own sites, something normally managed under the umbrella of the local authority itself. Therefore the design and updating of the site is often managed centrally by the authority technical staff, allowing the librarian limited scope in developing content. The use of content management systems can get over this problem, allowing a uniform look to be adopted and text to be updated by nominated staff in each local authority department.

An excellent example of what can be achieved by a library service in control of its own web presence is illustrated by Gateshead Council's iKnow service (www.asaplive.com/). This site is a detailed information gateway into services offered by the library and other high quality information sources.

Conclusion

The role of the public library in information provision remains one of its most vital functions in society. The public should be assured that the information supplied via the public library is accurate, impartial and meets the needs of the user.

Increasingly reference-based services are moving to online delivery, mirroring the new publishing regimes of such materials. The growth of virtual reference services allows librarians to continue their excellent work in aiding library users in accessing quality information. Such services demand a broader understanding of people's information-seeking behaviour in this new environment.

Public librarians need to be aware of calls on them to limit access to specific kinds of information, and they must be prepared to challenge such demands if they are in any way inappropriate. The role of the librarian as a gatekeeper to information can be interpreted in two ways, as someone who opens the gate or as someone who wishes to close it. The democratic ideal demands that the library remains open to information seeking and free from anyone wishing to put unreasonable limits on what can be provided to the user.

References

Grogan, D. (1987) *Grogan's Case Studies in Reference Work, vol. 1,* Enquiries and the reference process, Clive Bingley.

Grogan, D. (1992) *Practical Reference Work,* 2nd edn, Library Association Publishing.

Hauptman, R. (1976) Professionalism or Culpability? An experiment in ethics, *Wilson Library Bulletin,* **50** (April), 626-7.

IFLA (2006) *Digital Reference Guidelines,* www.ifla.org/VII/s36/pubs/drg03.htm.

Information Services Group (1999) *Guidelines for Reference and Information Services in Public Libraries,* Library Association Publishing.

Juznic, P., Urbanija, J., Grabrijan, E., Miklavc, S., Oslaj, D. and Svoljsak, S. (2001) Excuse Me, How Do I Commit Suicide? Access to ethically disputed items of information in public libraries, *Library Management,* **22** (1/2), 75-80.

Kinnell, M. (ed.) (1992) *Informing Communities,* CSG Publishing.

Kovacs, D. (2007) *The Virtual Reference Handbook: interview and information delivery techniques for the chat and email environments,* Facet Publishing.

McMenemy, D., Poulter, A. and Burton, P. F. (2006) *A Handbook of Ethical Practice: a practical guide for dealing with ethical issues in information and library work,* Chandos.

Nicholson, D. and MacGregor, G. (2003) 'NOF-Digi': putting UK culture online, *OCLC Systems & Services,* **19** (3), 96-9.

SCONUL (2007) *Seven Pillars of Information Literacy*,
www.sconul.ac.uk/groups/information_literacy/sp/sp/
splancol.pdf.

Simmons, S. (ed.) (1993) *Civil Disasters: the role of the public libraries following a crisis in the community*, based on research by Marilyn Dover for the Department of National Heritage, Library Association Publishing.

Wilson, K. And Train, B. (2005) *Libraries are Good for Business*, Centre for the Public Library and information in Society, University of Sheffield.

Chapter 6

Lifelong learning

Introduction

Lifelong learning is the concept that learning is not something that is only undertaken within formal structures such as schools, colleges or universities, but that humans learn throughout their life, often informally, such as through reading a book, attending a seminar or watching a documentary, in addition to the formal learning they undertake at key stages of their life.

Public libraries are key facilitators in lifelong learning because:

- they are open to all citizens
- they provide access to a range of learning materials free
- they are easily accessible with relatively convenient opening hours
- they increasingly offer instructional courses using ICTs and partnerships.

This chapter will discuss the role of the public library in lifelong learning, the modern political aspects of the concept, and the pressures on library services as a result, and how public libraries have responded to the concept through specific service delivery.

What is lifelong learning?

Lifelong learning has been defined as 'a deliberate progression throughout the life of an individual, where the initial acquisition of knowledge and skills is reviewed and upgraded continuously, to meet challenges set by an ever-changing society' (Brophy, Fisher and Craven, 1998). It can be seen to be different from the structured learning which takes place in schools, further and higher education establishments. It is more informal in nature, can be picked up and completed at leisure and is learner-centred in that it can be engaged with in whichever way the learner desires.

Crucially conventional education is exclusive in nature, as progress normally requires prior qualifications; lifelong learning does not rely solely on qualification attainment and can be as meaningful to the learner in the form of attending short seminars or evening classes as it is in attending year-long certificate-bearing courses. The needs and wants of users vary at different parts of their life, and those providing lifelong learning recognize that informal learning may well be enough to satisfy a user need in some cases.

The specific concepts of lifelong learning and conventional education and their differences are elucidated clearly in a report entitled *Distributing the Library to the Learner* (Brophy, 1999). See Table 6.1.

Table 6.1 Conventional education and lifelong learning

Conventional education	Lifelong learning
One-off, discrete courses	Continuous activities
Knowledge transmission	Skills transmission
Formal	Informal
Institutional	Dispersed
Timetabled teaching	Any time/any place learning
Structured courses	'Bitty' modules
Teacher driven	Student driven
For individuals	Group learning as a social activity
Exclusive	Inclusive and pervasive

The public library and learning

The public library has always played an important role as an educational vehicle for the wider community. A key goal of the public library movement was to provide the population with the means to access materials that would help them self-educate; as Black has observed the 'history of the public library movement is riddled with the rhetoric of self-help' (Black, 1996, 163). It was believed that having access to learning materials would encourage people to better themselves.

The modern public library and lifelong learning

In its 2001 strategy document for centring the library as a key plank of lifelong learning policy, The Library Association highlighted what it believed to be the key offerings of the entire information and library sector:

- accessibility
- a supportive environment
- staff skilled in supporting learners and the learning process
- resources
- partnership and co-operation
- experience of strategic engagement.   (Library Association, 2001)

We have previously discussed other services that could come under the banner of lifelong learning, such as reader development and services for children and young people. Indeed many of the services provided under a reference library remit also could be deemed as serving a lifelong learning agenda:

> Librarians need to engage in all types of learning situations; they may assist learners by providing an information service about educational opportunities; an advisory service to discuss learning goals; and a referral service to learning opportunities outside the library or inside the library to independent study materials.
>
> (McNicol, 2002, 252)

Thus library staff need to develop a holistic knowledge of learning opportunities within their community. They need to be aware of not only any learning opportunities available within the library service itself, but also any in local colleges, or some way of accessing that data quickly and efficiently on behalf of the user. It is increasingly becoming the case that lifelong learning is seen as a specific service area in libraries, more often where organized instructional sessions such as classes in ICT or other events such as literacy classes are undertaken to support informal routes.

Staff roles

There is a key issue with regard to staffing roles in delivering lifelong learning. Public libraries need to be careful that they do not venture into areas they are not qualified to deliver, and they need to be aware of limitations in terms of staff skills. The largest body of staff in the public library are paraprofessionals, who are often not of a sufficient grade or training level to provide learning programmes. This is in addition to any formal training issues that should be considered. While the training undertaken through the People's Network qualified many members of staff to teach ICT skills to a low level, more specialized training should be considered for any more advanced classes that might be taught.

Another issue regarding staff that has been highlighted by Goulding relates to the desire in some to temper their enthusiasm for training users: 'Public library staff can be reluctant to become engaged in user training. Underconfident of their own skills and with some novice users requiring considerable support, staff with other demands on their time can be reluctant to provide extensive advice and guidance to users' (Goulding, 2006, 177).

There is also the issue of being able to support the training via staff resources. Unless extra finance has been forthcoming librarians can find themselves attempting to run traditional services as well as provide time-consuming ICT support, and this can have a negative impact on services in other areas. The reality is that to provide high quality training for users who wish to use ICT facilities requires dedicated staff, or enhanced numbers of staff on duty to be able to cover any shortfall.

Spacey and Goulding emphasize that public library staff need several skills to be effective in offering advice regarding learning opportunities:

■ knowledge of the local and national educational climate

- understanding of adult learners' needs
- recognition and understanding of the library's own policy regarding learners. (Spacey and Goulding, 2004, 344)

UK policy background

The first key government policy document that has influenced the growth of lifelong learning within the UK was published in 1998, one year after the New Labour Government took office. Entitled *The Learning Age: a renaissance for a new Britain*, the green paper argued that the country 'will need a workforce with imagination and confidence, and the skills required will be diverse' (DfEE, 1998).

Since *The Learning Age* several other policy documents have emerged related to lifelong learning policy in the UK. *Skills for Life* aimed to create achievable targets for literacy and numeracy levels in the period 2001-4 (DfEE, 2001). In their foreword to *21st Century Skills: realising our potential*, Tony Blair and his ministers suggest that 'We must motivate and support many more learners to re-engage in learning. For too many people, learning is something that stops when they leave school. Learning new skills, at work and for pleasure, must become a rewarding part of everyday life' (DfES, 2003).

It is exactly this kind of vision, encouraging adults to re-engage in learning, be it formal or informal, that places the public library at the heart of the lifelong learning agenda. Complementing the existing formal provision in terms of schools and further education colleges, public libraries can offer a pathway back into learning for many people who have perhaps felt that it was no longer for them, either as an informal venue, or as a source of learning materials.

An important development in the Government's lifelong learning agenda was the creation of the University for Industry, or UfI (in Scotland this was known as the Scottish University for Industry, or SUfI). The emphasis of the UfI was creating a system whereby people could reskill for new work challenges that would face them in the 21st century. The major public face of the initiative was the learndirect brand, which is still in existence as a pathway into learning for many citizens. It offers a phone line and website where people can search for learning opportunities near them. As will be discussed below, the learndirect brand was also an important one for many public libraries.

Literacy and ICT literacy

Framework for the Future, as discussed in Chapter 1, placed libraries firmly at the heart of a drive towards enhancing lifelong learning and targeting illiteracies of all kinds. A startling statistic, for instance, was that 7 million adults in England had lower reading and writing levels than those expected of a child 11 years old. Placing a target date of 2007 to improve this for 1.5 million people, it suggested that public libraries were 'ideally placed to recognise and support people who might benefit from tuition' (DCMS, 2003, 8).

Literacy

Although it is certainly true that library staff are not normally qualified to teach literacy themselves, quite often the library can use partnerships to do so. Yet barriers exist for many potential users who may wish to improve their literacy through the library. McNicol highlights three main barriers that adult learners face in returning to learning:

■ *institutional*: over-bureaucratic systems, off-putting buildings, bad locations or inadequate facilities
■ *psychological*: bad memories of education from school; lack of confidence in abilities
■ *personal and social*: negativity of friends and family; gender role within cultural group seeing learning as not for you. (McNicol, 2002, 253)

Most notably the nature of the library itself is perhaps the main barrier to the learner seeking to improve their literacy skills; that is an institution that is built around providing services to the literate citizen. Although the potential cure for the problem may exist within the library's walls, the user may see the library as an inaccessible barrier in achieving that. Library catalogues, rules and regulations for joining, and knowing which books will help them and are written for their level can all be barriers for a citizen who is having problems with their literacy. They may be unable to admit their problem, and library staff need to have empathy with this position.

Train reported on the evaluation of a project designed to address some of the barriers adult learners may face when dealing with their literacy (Train, 2003). The Vital Link project aimed to link adult literacy and public libraries through a well designed reader development programme. Its objectives were:

■ to develop a major partnership programme harnessing libraries' reader development work to support adults trying to improve their literacy skills

■ to inspire, support and motivate emergent adult readers and recruit new 'hard to reach' learners

■ to establish effective links between the library service and the adult basic education sector

■ to identify, evaluate and articulate the unique contribution libraries' reader development work can make to the Government's plans to improve basic literacy skills

■ to research, implement and disseminate replicable local models at regional and national levels

■ to provide a range of support strategies and materials collections during and following the programme. (Train, 2003, 396)

As we previously discussed in Chapter 4, reader development is reader-centred, not about the author, theme or genre of the book. Thus reaching adult learners with such a programme can be achieved by using a policy of selecting materials that they will enjoy and that will encourage them to read.

Addressing literacy issues in library users can successfully be undertaken via partnerships involving the library and services providing adult tutors. This is often undertaken through community education departments in the local authority, but is also frequently done via further education colleges supplying tutors for classes or one-on-one sessions with learners within the library.

ICTs and lifelong learning

Lifelong learning opportunities are greatly enhanced by the availability of ICTs in libraries. As well as the wide range of materials on CD-ROM and DVD-ROM that can be purchased to offer interactive learning opportunities, many formal courses can now be taught online and used via public library computer terminals. Access to online learning was one of the key strands of the People's Network programme which saw a national infrastructure of ICT equipment installed in public libraries, as well as significant investment in staff training.

ICT skills

A key literacy for the 21st century has been and will be computer literacy. Although young children and younger people born within the period of the growth of the internet feel competent and skilled in accessing this world, many in other age groups do not and are thus disenfranchised from the process.

ICT skills are now essential in the population simply because much of the world is now accessed via the internet. For instance e-government becomes inaccessible if a citizen cannot use a computer, and this cuts off access to politicians and government departments. Many of the basic services delivered by local and central government are now delivered via e-government, and have been since 2005.

As Goulding discusses, a great deal of the lifelong learning agenda 'in public libraries has focussed initially on enhancing people's basic ICT skills in recognition of the fact that they need to be able to use technology competently before they can access the other benefits that it brings' (Goulding, 2006, 175).

Todd and Tedd reported on an initiative undertaken in Belfast that sought to encourage library users to sign up for formal ICT qualifications in the library, namely Computer Literacy and Information Technology (CLAIT) and the European Computer Driving Licence (ECDL) (Todd and Tedd, 2000). This was a pattern followed by many public library services, which signed up as test centres for courses like the ECDL, helping them achieve two goals: the opportunity to offer formal qualifications to users in addition to the informal learning opportunities, and to raise revenue through the test and course fees that could be charged. Becoming an ECDL test centre involved accreditation through the British Computer Society, the organization that administered the test.

Hawkey discusses the greater aims of lifelong learning and the potential ICT has in delivering it:

> if learning is to be more than the transmission, receipt and assimilation of knowledge, then the programme for lifelong learning cannot simply comprise action replays of earlier pedagogic encounters. There is an alternative approach, with an emphasis on participation, democracy and decision making. Rather than sitting in the stands, or cheering from the touch-line, ICT will enable learners to acquire transferable skills and to play a full part in the game, according to their own rules.
>
> (Hawkey, 2002, 5)

As discussed earlier, public libraries have traditionally been places in which users could pursue learning and self-development; ICT-based learning or e-learning is simply a new way in which this can be facilitated and delivered. The main challenge now for library staff is to ensure that support and advice are accessible where and when they are needed.

Public library initiatives

There is no single model for how public libraries have adopted the concept of lifelong learning for their members. Certainly as a political priority all public libraries aim to meet this community need, but the actual delivery in terms of how this is achieved is very different across the country. We have highlighted above some of the initiatives that have seen public libraries engage learners within their communities but they are by no means exhaustive as the literature on public library lifelong learning initiatives is growing as librarians seek to publish their findings on various aspects of their service delivery. A useful publication for seeking out the most up to date information on lifelong learning initiatives in libraries is the *Public Library Journal*, published by the Public Libraries Group, a special interest group of CILIP.

The section below will briefly highlight some other early initiatives that were adopted in light of the lifelong learning agenda.

SAILS (Staff Development for Access to Information and Learning in Sunderland) project

The SAILS project was an initiative in the north east of England whereby the three main library sectors in the city formed a partnership to give all members of each institution access to the collections of the partners. This meant that the university, colleges and public libraries were all accessible to members of any of the other institutions, creating a network of 29 libraries for members. A key emphasis of the project was the role of staff development across the sectors to enable high quality provision regardless of the type of library the adult learners used.

Real: lifelong learning

Another initiative that brought education providers and the public library service to work together was the Real: lifelong learning programme in Glasgow. The partnership also involved the local enterprise company and local businesses.

The project involved all the local community libraries in the city rebranding themselves under the Real banner, while retaining their library identity. The branding was consistently applied so that public libraries and businesses who installed Real learning centres all had similar interior design and use of logos and promotional materials.

A key part of the programme was the development of online learning opportunities in the form of learning bites, which were short online tutorials aimed at improving basic skills, for example by giving tips on communication or how to be a learner.

Learndirect centres

Learndirect is the Government's skills and training advisory body. Citizens can call or visit the website to obtain information on courses and other training opportunities. As part of the initiative libraries and other organizations that offered formal and informal training were able to apply for learndirect branding to become a learndirect centre.

This made the public libraries involved part of a national initiative and a potential venue for learning for anyone who called the learndirect advice line for information on a course. This enabled public libraries to market themselves more widely to potential learners who may not be aware of the opportunities available within the library, thus reaching out to non-users.

Conclusion

Lifelong learning became a key plank in UK government policy from 1998 onwards and influenced the design and development of public library services in the era afterwards. Public libraries throughout the UK have embraced the concept of lifelong learning and sought to ensure that they provided high quality lifelong learning opportunities for their users.

The various initiatives discussed above illustrate that lifelong learning is a continuous service strand for public libraries across the UK. It is in this area that we can perceive the links back to the old mechanics' institutes that formed so many of the early public library collections and the mantra of self-help so evident in the goals of the original framers of public library legislation. We can see that public libraries have always supported the lifelong learner in society, long before the term became prominent politically. It is no surprise to see public libraries politically strengthened through their association with this key government policy.

The end result has been a movement in some authorities towards offering accredited qualifications for users undertaking learning within the library. Although this model is by no means universal, it opens up exciting opportunities for public libraries to extend their role within their communities. It also offers the opportunity for disadvantaged members of a community to re-enter learning in a more informal way, creating the bridge of confidence that may have been barring their entry to formal qualifications.

References

Black, A. (1996) *A New History of the English Public Library: social and intellectual contexts, 1850–1914*, Leicester University Press.
Brophy, P. (1999) *Distributing the Library to the Learner*, CERLIM,

www.ukoln.ac.uk/services/papers/bl/blri078/content/
repor~22.htm.

Brophy, P., Fisher, S. and Craven, J. (1998) *The Development of UK Academic Library Services in the Context of Lifelong Learning: final report*,
www.ukoln.ac.uk/services/elib/papers/tavistock/ukals/ukals.pdf.

DCMS (2003) *Framework for the Future: libraries, learning and information in the next decade*, Department for Culture, Media and Sport.

DfEE (1998) *The Learning Age: a renaissance for a new Britain*, Department for Education and Employment,
www.lifelonglearning.co.uk/greenpaper/index.htm.

DfEE (2001) *Skills for Life - the national strategy for improving adult literacy and numeracy skills: delivering the vision 2001-2004*, Department for Education and Employment,
www.dcsf.gov.uk/readwriteplus/bank/ACF35CE.pdf.

DfES (2003) *21st Century Skills: realising our potential*, Department for Education and Skills,
www.dcsf.gov.uk/skillsstrategy/uploads/documents/
21st%20Century%20Skills.pdf.

Goulding, A. (2006) *Public Libraries in the 21st Century: defining services and debating the future*, Ashgate.

Hawkey, R. (2002) The Lifelong Learning Game: season ticket or free transfer?, *Computers & Education*, **38**, 5-20.

Library Association (2001) *Libraries and Lifelong Learning: a strategy 2002-2004*, Library Association.

McNicol, S. (2002) Learning in Libraries: lessons for staff, *New Library World*, **103** (1178/1179), 251-8.

Spacey, R. and Goulding, A. (2004) Learner Support in UK Public Libraries, *Aslib Proceedings: new information perspectives*, **56** (6), 344-55.

Todd, M. and Tedd, L. A. (2000) Training Courses for ICT as Part of Lifelong Learning in Public Libraries: experiences with a pilot scheme in Belfast Public Libraries, *Program*, **34** (4), 375-83.

Train, B. (2003) Building Up or Breaking Down Barriers? The role of the public library in adult basic skills education, *Library Review*, **52** (8), 394-402.

Part 3

Issues in management and service development

Chapter 7

The impact of information and communications technology

Introduction

Information and communications technologies (ICTs) have had a dramatic influence on society, and the way people use public libraries. In fact technology has been a key driver in service development across library sectors for decades, but the advent of the internet and the world wide web (WWW) has begun to change the way the public use and interact with information, and as a consequence how they expect some services to be delivered.

This chapter will discuss the impact ICTs have had on public libraries, how they are altering how many traditional services are being provided, and what this means for the public librarian charged with managing these developments.

Understanding the use of technology in libraries

The term ICT is a relatively new acronym for describing computer technologies, replacing the term IT (information technology), which was used for decades. The addition of the communications tag has largely been the result of the ability to use the same technologies for communicating with others via the internet. The terms tend to be interchangeable for many people, and thus it is common to hear people still refer to IT. Indeed in the USA it is common to find professionals in information and library work who do not use the term ICT and continue to use IT to describe the technologies.

ICTs can be found in many aspects of the modern public library service. In Chapter 3 we discussed equity of access, and indeed public libraries remain crucial gateways for many people to access ICTs who otherwise could not afford to do so. Yet long before the first library user interacted with a computer in the public library, the technologies that underpin them had been transforming how the services they used were delivered.

The library management system

The gateway to the library's collections is the catalogue, more often than not nowadays in the form of an online public access catalogue, or OPAC. The OPAC can be accessed within the library building, and for most public library systems in the developed world, via the internet using the website of the public library authority concerned. Indeed, in the UK this latter access was a cornerstone of e-government expectations for local authorities.

The library management system (LMS) is the most important technological tool in the library; it manages the important data used in the day to day operations such as user membership records, borrowed items, borrowing entitlements and periods, and fines. Modern LMS solutions tend to be modular in nature, meaning that after buying the basic catalogue system a service is able to add extra functionality that can control other aspects of the work of the library, such as:

- ordering and acquisitions
- serials control
- management information (usage statistics, etc.)
- revenue control (for collecting fines, sales monies, etc.).

Many also offer modules that can create digital libraries, or more interactive spaces for users; however, each module added is an extra expense for the library and may require more assistance from the IT support staff.

CD-ROMs and databases

In the 1980s CD-ROMs became important information storage and delivery tools. The ability to store databases containing bibliographic, indexing and abstracting tools that had been the staple of libraries for many years, such as *Library and Information Science Abstracts*, *British Humanities Index*, *Books in Print* and numerous other titles, was the first sign that traditional ways of delivering some library services were now under challenge. Add to this the ability to store full text databases containing many years of journals, newspapers, poetry and other texts, and it was clear that, from a user standpoint, access to resources was to become quicker and more efficient.

As technology evolved the media used by companies to store their services also evolved. After CD-ROMs came DVD-ROMs, able to store around ten times as much as a CD-ROM, but increasingly access to databases and electronic services became internet-based, and this is now the norm for subscription services.

Subscriptions to electronic services

Local authorities have been using the benefits of consortia purchasing for some time, offering opportunities to gain large discounts by collectively using specific suppliers. This is a useful strategy from the point of view of online subscription services, as it can be a challenge, both to understand pricing schemes when negotiating licences for such products, and to afford to pay for them.

In Scotland an early model of adoption used left-over monies from the country's People's Network allocation to provide access to three services: Kompass UK, Know UK, and Newsbank (Kerr, 2003). These three services provided access to a wealth of reference information, for example on UK companies, and a range of standard reference information on UK issues, and subscription to electronic back copies of newspapers.

Recently in England the MLA has negotiated with a range of electronic service providers to offer a framework agreement that all public library services can use under its Reference Online scheme (MLA, 2008). Services available include many standard reference sources traditionally subscribed to by libraries including the *Oxford Dictionary of National Biography*, the

Oxford English Dictionary Online and *Grove Music* and *Grove Art*. A full list of all services covered by the agreement is available at the Reference Online scheme website (MLA, 2008).

Crucially such agreements make some of the most authoritative reference sources available to some smaller libraries which could perhaps not have afforded to purchase the hard copies. Some of the licences for electronic services also permit library users to access the services at home after keying in their library card details. The availability of electronic reference services is thus one of the key areas where ICTs are significantly enhancing the quality of service provision for library users.

E-books and e-serials

Researchers at the University of Loughborough have conducted recent studies into the use of electronic books (e-books) and electronic serials (e-serials) within public libraries.

One project set up and evaluated the introduction of an e-books service in Essex. The provision included:

- lending iPAQ personal digital assistant (PDA) devices with a number of e-book titles loaded, to specific groups of users
- providing PC-based web access to two e-book collections to a range of library patrons. Users were offered e-books for download based on Adobe 6 and Palm e-book formats (Dearnley et al., 2004, 6).

The project found that users were critical of the hardware used to deliver the e-books, in particular of the screen, text and battery life of PDAs. One respondent noted that it was impossible to take one into the bath unlike a printed book (Dearnley et al., 2004, 21). Overall the study found that it was not altogether impossible to imagine that libraries might provide e-books, but thought would need to be given to the appropriate hardware models and funding regimes to allow users to access the digital content.

The data gathered by the researchers for the project on e-serials showed that many public libraries subscribed to them, with 71% of library authorities subscribing to an e-serial in the period when the study was undertaken (Dearnley et al., 2004, 10). However libraries only subscribed to a few services: 53% subscribed to two services, 17% to three services and 10% to four services.

A study by Ball in 2003 found that public libraries were successfully negotiating consortia purchasing in the e-services and e-serials marketplace. Dearnley et al. suggested that such purchasing arrangements have created blanket coverage of subscriptions in Northern Ireland and Wales (Dearnley et al., 2004, 26).

The People's Network

The single largest influence on the development of ICTs in UK public libraries has been the People's Network programme. In just five years it transformed the network and equipment infrastructure and skills levels of staff in public libraries across the country. The project led to all UK public libraries being provided with computers and high-speed internet access. The project was completed on time and within budget in 2002.

Background and aims of the programme

The key document that started the process was the 1997 Library and Information Commission report, *New Library: the People's Network*. It stated:

> Tomorrow's new library will be a key agent in enabling people of all ages to prosper in the information society – helping them acquire new skills for employment, use information creatively, and improve the quality of their lives. Libraries will play a central role in the University for Industry, in lifelong learning projects, and in support of any individual who undertakes self-development.
>
> (Library and Information Commission, 1997)

The aim of the programme was to create the infrastructure, content and staff skills to support a new networked public library. Funding for the programme to the tune of £100 million was allocated from the New Opportunities Fund (NOF), which was part of the National Lottery programme, with additional support from the Bill and Melinda Gates Foundation.

Staff skills in delivering ICT services

Fundamental to the success of the project was a nationwide training programme incorporating all frontline library staff. Within the allocated funding for each local authority was a sum of money that was to be used directly for the training of staff; the sum for the entire country totalled £20 million.

The follow-up report *Building the New Library Network* advocated eight training outcomes it deemed necessary for public libraries:

- competence with ICT
- understanding how ICT can support library work
- health, safety and legal issues relating to ICT
- using ICT to find information for users (including evaluating information)
- using ICT to support reader development
- using ICT to support users to ensure effective learning
- effective management of ICT resources
- knowing how to use ICT to improve efficiency.

(Library and Information Commission, 1998)

The first outcome was deemed to be the minimum level that all staff working in public libraries should have as standard. The solution adopted by the majority of public libraries was to use the competencies inherent in the European Computer Driving Licence (ECDL) as the benchmark for the first outcome, which was based around competence in computing applications. This ensured that all staff were trained in word processing, web browsing, spreadsheets and databases, and had an overview of computing basics like hardware and software, and managing files and desktops. The more advanced outcomes were covered by more specialized training courses such as the Diploma in Applications of ICT in Libraries and the Advanced Diploma in Applications of ICT in Libraries developed in Scotland by the Scottish Library and Information Council under the banner of the Scottish Qualifications Authority.

For most authorities the challenge of training staff was considerable; freeing staff time to undertake training was perhaps the biggest challenge. Certainly the training programme was unprecedented and massively upskilled an entire workforce in a relatively short space of time. A 1999 study suggested, however, that the skills of the staff in the new library would be only partly based around ICT skills, and that the new demands placed on the service necessitated staff skilled in outreach and education, and helping learners use ICTs for their benefit (Jones et al., 1999). As discussed in Chapter 6 this can certainly be seen to be the case as public libraries increasingly provide learning opportunities for users through their new facilities and offer enhanced staff development through their ability to help learners.

Evaluation of the project

By 2004 there were over 30,000 personal computers available in public libraries in England and Wales, with an average of seven computers per library (Brophy, 2004, 21), and this was a monumental improvement on the situation before the People's Network was implemented. Not only the numbers of computers but also the speed of connection meant that all libraries were offering high speed and high quality ICT access to their users, allowing the most up to date uses possible of facilities, including enhanced multimedia access.

Sustainability of ICTs

The issue of sustainability of ICT equipment will be discussed more fully in Chapter 8. The key issue to consider with regard to the People's Network was that it was a one-off grant that allowed for the purchase of one iteration only of equipment for each library service. Thus sustainability became a major concern for each individual library authority and it was no surprise to see some public libraries beginning to charge users to access ICT equipment when the funding cycle was complete. Regrettable as this is, the reality is that the expense of regularly replacing an entire ICT infrastructure to keep the equipment up to the standards users need and expect will be an ongoing challenge.

Public access computing

The nature of the internet and some of the information contained on it makes for some potential ethical and logistical problems for public libraries in terms of what can be accessed by users using their computers. Measures to control how users interact with the internet while in the public library have been brought in across the country, and this has included developing acceptable use policies (AUPs) that each user or parent of a child using the internet has to agree to before being given internet access.

The purpose of an AUP is to define what constitutes acceptable use of the library facilities. This is a useful management tool for many public libraries, but at its root it challenges the principle of providing equity of access, since it defines some information as inappropriate. This is entirely understandable when the issue of child protection is the goal; no right-minded individual would wish children to be exposed to pornographic content when visiting their public library. However many policies define sites such as chat rooms, gambling sites and games sites as being inappropriate, and this is where the choice about what to block becomes potentially problematic.

It is often posited that libraries should move with the times, and as people become more and more familiar with the many uses of the internet, the bar on anything but information use within a library becomes difficult to sustain ethically. Sites such as Facebook, Bebo and MySpace are enormously popular with young people, a group of users who are notoriously hard to reach with marketing. Libraries that restrict access to sites such as these run the risk of alienating this group of users.

The second measure introduced by many public libraries, and perhaps the most controversial, is the software-based solution of internet filtering. While AUPs define in a general fashion what is and is not acceptable use of the internet, filtering software goes a step further and blocks any information it is programmed to block, either by using keywords, or a list of banned addresses, or a combination of both. Although it is true that, as Hauptman puts it, 'unfiltered access to the Internet presents some major ethical challenges even to those whose commitment to intellectual freedom is unequivocal', it is equally true that 'it is not our business to mediate between users and the virtual world' (Hauptman, 2002, 65).

Public libraries ventured down the filtering route to protect themselves and their users rather than in a bid to halt intellectual freedom, but this makes the decision even more problematic for an ethical public librarian.

The problem with filtering is that although it may block material that is offensive or questionable (though the question of to whom it is offensive remains), it has also been found to block material of a legitimate nature, and often this material is of personal or sensitive importance to a user, such as health information or information on sexuality.

It could be argued that it is the clumsiness of filtering software that poses the largest ethical concern; it will never be 100% accurate, even if it ever becomes 99.9% accurate. Taking the human out of assessing information for a user is always a bad thing, but to put it in the hands of a software program is a clumsy solution to the problem. Combating the ignorance of many stakeholders with regard to the accuracy of filtering is also a challenge of the 21st century facing public librarians. When and if inappropriate access occurs it can cause controversy for the library, and an organization that feels it is protected is one operating under a false sense of security. As Gorman succinctly puts it, 'the truth is that filtering systems *do not work* and they *never will work!*'(Gorman, 2000, 96).

Whether introduced willingly or unwillingly, the use of filtering technologies in libraries of any kind is a major ethical concern. Regardless of which side a public librarian comes down on in the debate, it is essential that everyone is aware of all the implications that using the software may bring when making a decision to install or not.

Managing access

Another major challenge that was exacerbated with the People's Network revolution was managing access to the ICTs within the library. Many libraries went from a minimal ICT infrastructure to one that took up much staff time to ensure efficient operation. Managing access took on three important considerations:

- how to manage the volume of users requesting access, and ensuring fair usage of ICTs
- how to ensure that ICTs were not abused or altered by mischievous users
- how to keep ICTs equipped with the most up to date patches and plug-ins.

Booking systems

The administration of ICTs in public libraries is a logistical challenge for even the smallest library. A library with six computers that is open for ten hours daily may see anything up to 20 users per computer per day if they use 30-minute booking slots. This amounts to 120 potential users who have to be logged on and off from a computer. This is in addition to any assistance they may require and the need to keep operating the traditional service in unison.

A common solution libraries have adopted has been to purchase a software system that can handle bookings of ICT equipment. A popular choice has been Netloan, which was a package originally developed by a Swedish software company to manage the bookings of bowling alley lanes.

Its use as a computer booking system has been widely embraced by public libraries in the UK as it offers useful service enhancements, such as the ability to manage printing and bookings for computers via the internet. This means that a library user can be in their workplace or school and book a slot for themselves in their local library at a time convenient to them without visiting the library or calling it. All that is normally needed is the library barcode number and PIN, as the Netloan system interfaces with LMS data to authenticate the user.

Protecting the computer

As the numbers of computers in libraries increased, so did the potential for users who wished to sabotage the equipment. In a standard computer the operating system and hard drives are open to any user unless an administrator has restricted functionality. The safest way to do this is to employ a software or hardware-based system to make the computer tamper-proof. These generally work by making a mirror of the computer hard drive which is hidden from public view and which boots up every time the computer is switched on. Such a set up means that any tampering with the configuration, either malicious or accidental, is automatically wiped when the system is reset.

Although an added expense, in a public access computing environment such expense is essential and saves on computer downtime significantly.

Plug-ins

A plug-in is a piece of software that works with a web browser to allow specific types of content to be displayed or heard on a computer. Examples of common plug-ins are Quicktime, Windows Media Player and Macromedia Flash.

It is a key challenge for public libraries to ensure that their ICTs are able to deliver the most up to date multimedia content. More and more websites are using higher bandwidth availability and offering multimedia as standard, and sites like the BBC offer excellent quality in so doing. Yet if the correct plug-in is not available on a library computer then the user may be unable to access the content.

Keeping plug-ins up to date is not a straightforward task if a library computer uses software like Deep Freeze and the staff on the ground are not able or not authorized to update the computers. This can lead to IT staff employed by the library having to undertake upgrades of such things themselves, and they may not do this as frequently as is required. Solutions exist, such as updating remotely, but whichever way is chosen to upgrade the plug-ins in question, it remains an ongoing concern as new plug-ins are released frequently and many content providers choose to adopt the latest iterations for creating their content.

Technology-enhanced services

ICTs also offer public libraries exciting opportunities to provide new ways of accessing current information. As well as subscription-based services discussed earlier, some traditional library services are now also able to be delivered electronically.

Digitization

Digitization is literally the act of taking a physical analogue item and creating a digital facsimile of it. This is distinct from material that is already born-digital, such as word-processed documents, spreadsheets and the like.

Digitization initiatives in public libraries were significantly boosted by the NOF-Digitise programme, which ran alongside the People's Network initiative to ensure that as well as a physical infrastructure there would also be content for library users to access. The resulting web portal,

Enrich UK, gave access to all of the websites funded under the programme. The Enrich UK portal has now been subsumed by the larger EU-wide programme MICHAEL (Multilingual Inventory of Cultural Heritage in Europe) and is available via the MLA website.

The NOF-Digitise programme was a major catalyst in giving many public libraries a first taste of digitization and digital content creation. Since most public libraries have collections that are worth digitizing from both local and national standpoints, digitization in library services is certain to have an ongoing role.

Websites

All public library services in the UK now have websites, and the entire list can be accessed via the useful website constructed by Sheila and Robert Harden (Harden and Harden, 2008). As mentioned above it was a requirement of public libraries as part of their e-government responsibilities to the local authority to make their library catalogue available through their website.

The challenge for the public library is to balance its e-government goal as a department within a local authority versus its information-based role to provide gateways for users to information. This is a crucial point if the library webpage is used as the first screen a user sees when logging on to a library computer, as happens in many authorities throughout Britain.

Badly designed sites can alter the experience and efficiency of the user's searching, and public libraries should always seek to ensure that these pages are constructed with the information goals of the user in mind rather than the e-government agenda of the local authority. In a small scale study conducted by this author it was found that only one library authority of 12 visited offered a novice guide to the internet as part of their pages for instance (McMenemy, 2007). This meant any novice users would be reliant on staff availability or some other materials being available within the library in order to undertake a self-directed learning opportunity on the computer.

Web 2.0

The most recent major innovation in electronic services is known as Web 2.0, which enhances traditional internet-based services by encouraging more user interaction and input. One of the main advocates of Web 2.0 describes it thus:

> Web 2.0 is the network as platform, spanning all connected devices; Web 2.0 applications are those that make the most of the intrinsic advantages of that platform; delivering software as a continually-updated service that gets the better the more people use it, consuming and remixing data from multiple sources, including individual users, while providing their own data and services in a form that allows remixing by others, creating network effects through an 'architecture of participation', and going beyond the page metaphor of Web 1.0 to deliver rich user experiences.
>
> (O'Reilly, 2005)

The most famous incarnations of the phenomenon are commercial sites such as MySpace and Facebook, but public libraries have sought to enter the domain too. East Renfrewshire Council was the first authority in the UK to create Facebook pages for all of its community libraries (Browne and Rooney-Browne, 2008) in a bid to reach out to those who may well be Facebook users, but not library users. Although still in its infancy, the project found that the library service widened its reach significantly, 'not only from East Renfrewshire and surrounding areas but also from Australia, London, Oklahoma, Saudi Arabia and Toronto' (Browne and Rooney-Browne, 2008, 15).

Conclusion

ICTs are now a crucial component in many of the services provided by modern public libraries. They greatly enhance user services in areas of reference work and in digitization of library materials such as photographic collections. However, they have not and will not for the foreseeable future replace many of the core public library activities.

Despite the obvious current interest in e-books, books in this form are unlikely in the short term to replace traditional books to any significant degree, except in the areas of reference or scholarly publishing where currency and multiple access issues remain of paramount importance. This may well change as technology improves and developers find more efficient and user friendly ways of displaying the written word electronically; the Amazon Kindle e-book reader currently popular in the USA is a sign that technology in this area is moving on. However, for many users the pleasure of reading is in the touch and feel of the written word on paper and this is unlikely ever to be bettered by technology.

Of all professions it is perhaps librarianship that sees the most debate between those who advocate the use of ICTs, and those who do not see ICTs as being central functions of their service, or worse detrimental to them. At times there almost seems to be a crisis of professional identity, with many advocating traditional library services over new, and vice versa. In reality the modern public library service must use electronic services where they enhance the service provided to the user, but they should not pursue an ICT agenda for the sake of it, and certainly not at the expense of traditional services and traditional users.

It is unprofessional for any librarian to inhabit a camp that promotes either technophobia or technophilia at the expense of service development for the user. The reality is that in the 21st century there are many services that are much more successfully delivered via ICTs, and there are many that are not and are unlikely ever to be so. Taking a view on one side or the other is a straightforward way to curry favour from one of the particular camps, but it does little to move services forward for users and even less to meet their actual needs. If we allow our prejudices regarding format to colour our professional judgement we will have failed the users in our service to them.

References

Ball, D. (2003) Public Libraries and the Consortium Purchase of Electronic Resources, *The Electronic Library*, **21** (4), 301–9.

Brophy, P. (2004) *The People's Network: moving forward*, Museums, Libraries and Archives.

Browne, A. and Rooney-Browne, C. (2008) Punching Above Our
    Weight: a small Scottish library service joins the global
    community, *World Library and Information Congress, 74th IFLA
    General Conference and Council*, 10–14 August, Québec, Canada,
    www.ifla.org/IV/ifla74/papers/159-Browne_Rooney-Browne-
    en.pdf.
Dearnley, J., Berube, L. and Palmer, M. (2004) *Electronic Books in Public
    Libraries: a feasibility study for developing usage models for web-based
    and hardware-based electronic books*, Department of Information
    Science, Loughborough.
Dearnley, J., Towle, G., Dungworth, N. and McKnight, C. (2006) *E-
    Serial Provision in UK Public Libraries: a survey of issues and
    practice*, Department of Information Science, Loughborough.
Gorman, M. (2000) *Our Enduring Values: librarianship in the 21st
    century*, American Library Association.
Harden, S. and Harden, R. (2008) *UK Public Libraries*,
    http://dspace.dial.pipex.com/town/square/ac940/ukpublib.html.
Hauptman, R. (2002) *Ethics and Librarianship*, McFarland and Co.
Jones, B., Sprague, M., Nankivell, C. and Richter, K. (1999) *Staff in the
    New Library: skills, needs and learning choices*, British Library
    Research and Innovation Centre.
Kerr, G. (2003) Value Added Facts, *Information Scotland*, **1** (1),
    February,
    www.slainte.org.uk/publications/serials/infoscot/vol1(1)/
    value.html.
Library and Information Commission (1997) *New Library: the People's
    Network*.
Library and Information Commission (1998) *Building the New Library
    Network*.
McMenemy, D. (2007) Internet Access: an uneven picture, *Library and
    Information Update*, October,
    www.cilip.org.uk/publications/updatemagazine/archive/
    archive2007/october/McMenemyoct07.htm.
Miller, P. (2005) Web 2.0: building the new library, *Ariadne*, **45**,
    www.ariadne.ac.uk/issue45/miller/intro.html.

MLA (2008) *MLA Programmes: reference online,*
www.mla.gov.uk/programmes/digital_initiatives/reference_
online.

O'Reilly, T. (2005) Web 2.0: compact definition?, *O'Reilly Radar blog,*
http://radar.oreilly.com/archives/2005/10/web_20_compact_
definition.html.

Chapter 8

Management, governance and budgeting issues

Introduction

Like all organizations public libraries need an appropriate management structure in place to ensure services are delivered and developed and in order for the resources provided by the community to be properly accounted for. In addition public libraries in the UK are operated under the banner of local authorities and as a result do not deliver their services in a vacuum; thus libraries must support the strategic objectives of an umbrella organization that has a wide range of statutory responsibilities and only a finite budget to respond to them.

This chapter will discuss some of the key governance issues facing public libraries in the modern era, such as:

- local authority structures and reorganization
- the place of the public library in the local authority structure
- management and budgeting
- income generation
- partnership working
- recent management trends.

Local authorities

In the UK public library services are delivered by local authorities. It is a statutory requirement for local authorities in England and Wales to provide a library service under the 1964 Public Libraries and Museums Act. In Scotland the Act relating to public libraries is the Local Government (Scotland) Act 1973. Although the local authority structure ensures that public libraries are delivered for local needs, under the provisions of the 1964 Act the Secretary of State for Culture has ultimate responsibility for public libraries and all local authorities have to ensure that the libraries they administer meet the standards specified by the Department for Culture, Media and Sport. Similarly in Scotland as public libraries are under the devolved administration's remit the ultimate responsibility for them is in the hands of the local government minister, who is responsible to the Scottish Parliament.

Local authority governance

A local authority is a statutory body charged with administering local services for a specific geographic community. Normally called councils, they consist of:

- *Councillors*: elected through ballots in local areas defined as wards. One councillor is normally elected by the body of councillors to become mayor, or in Scotland Lord Provost.
- *Committees*: made up of a subset of councillors, related to a specific service theme, e.g. licensing, culture, education. Committees are normally charged with budgeting and decision making on these areas, which then have to be rubber stamped by the full council. Senior officials of the departments advise the committees.
- *Departments*: increasingly have become larger umbrella departments that are responsible to the specific committee for that service area, for instance an education department may be responsible for schools, nurseries, community education initiatives and libraries.
- *Officials*: salaried employees responsible for the provision of services within a council. This runs from senior officials, such as heads of service

or their senior management team, down to lower-ranked professionals such as team or assistant librarians.

Councils are financed by money allocated to them through both central taxation and a local council tax. Notwithstanding the importance of council tax, financially and politically, the vast majority of funding for a local authority comes from central taxation and thus national accountability is of importance as well as local accountability.

The services administered by councils are wide, varying from schools to libraries and museums, to cleansing and refuse, social work, environmental health and licensing. This means that the umbrella organization that administers the public library system has a wide range of responsibilities that do not always appear on the surface to be linked, other than that they are provided for the same geographical group of people. Thus public libraries are competing with many other public services to access appropriate funds, making advocacy from within the public libraries and the wider profession a vital component of service development.

Political dimensions

As local authorities are governed by an elected body of councillors, the main political parties in the UK are responsible for the vast majority of them. Because local authorities are elected the political persuasion of the elected body of the council may vary from council to council, and often the political party that is in control of central government is not in control of a local authority. Therefore political tensions may exist between the goals of the elected members on the local council and those of the central government.

Usherwood's 1993 study of elected members' viewpoints on libraries clearly illustrated that the party affiliation of the member governed in many ways how they saw the library service. In the early 1990s there was regular debate about the value of contracting out public services to the private sector, and the policy of compulsory competitive tendering was a political hot potato. Usherwood's interviews revealed at the time that Conservative councillors were far more likely to back calls for public libraries to charge for services or contract them out than their counterparts of a Labour or Liberal Democrat persuasion (Usherwood, 1993).

Clearly while the independence of the profession and its ethical code suggests that public librarians should not ally themselves with any particular political party, it is nonetheless clear that the political priorities of elected administrations will influence service delivery. In Chapter 3 we discussed the issue of social inclusion and its role as a key plank of New Labour public policy. Public libraries have been able to develop services that met this political policy, but it is questionable whether in doing so they have allied themselves to one political viewpoint over another. There is an inherent danger that with the removal of any administration, and the inevitable change in political and policy priorities that follows, a service seen to ally itself too closely with one party and its priorities runs the risk of becoming isolated when another takes power.

Local government reorganization

Finding the most efficient and appropriate model for the administration of local government in the UK is a challenge that has been attempted on several occasions in the past 30 or so years. The fact that the effort has not been repeated on more occasions than it has reflects the enormity of the task and the huge administrative burden that any major restructuring of local government brings with it. Clearly as public library services are part of the local government structure such changes have a direct impact on how they are managed and delivered.

History of reorganization

In modern times the major iterations of local government reorganization have taken place in the mid 1960s, the 1970s and the mid 1990s. Legislation that brought in reorganization in England was passed in 1972 and in Scotland in 1973. The legislation in both cases was influenced by a two-tier system of local government introduced into London in the mid 1960s. This two-tier system existed in the UK from the mid 1970s until the mid 1990s. The system split responsibility for different aspects of local government services to the two tiers. For example in Scotland, Edinburgh City Council operated services such as libraries, theatres and museums for its geographic area while Lothian Regional Council was responsible for services such as education across a wider area, which also took in several other councils.

The 1990s

The political viewpoint of the then Conservative Government during the 1990s was that the two-tier system that was introduced in the 1960s and 1970s was not the most efficient way of administering local authorities. Legislation was passed that created a single-tier system of local government in Scotland and Wales, although the English position was not so clear cut. The process of reorganization began in 1995 when the Isle of Wight became a unitary authority, although the next stage of change was more widespread, with Scotland and Wales seeing unitary authorities created across their areas, with a handful created in England in the initial phase, and more year on year.

Current position

Table 8.1 shows the current state of local government administration in the UK.

Table 8.1 Number of local authorities per country (Source: Office for National Statistics)	
Country	**Local authority types**
England	46 unitary authorities; 36 metropolitan districts; 36 shire counties
Northern Ireland	26 district councils
Scotland	32 unitary councils
Wales	22 unitary councils

How does the size of the authority influence service?

In 1994 while the then government was considering how to reorganize local government a study was undertaken into the best local authority model for delivering library services in terms of authority size. Much as McColvin had found 50 years previously, the authors of the report concluded that larger authorities had the best chance of offering an efficient model. They suggested that should the reorganization lead to a larger number of small authorities, then providing an acceptable level of service would cost more rather than less (Midwinter and McVicar, 1994, 72).

Departmental structures

With local government reorganization came the opportunity to streamline administration, and departments that were once distinct services were merged together into large umbrella departments. Libraries found services allocated under a diverse range of departments, including Community Services, Education, Culture and Leisure, among others.

Where libraries are placed in the hierarchy of a local authority may well have a bearing on how prominent they are within the minds of elected members when funding decisions are being made. Although it is clearly the duty of all staff to be determined advocates for their service, those at the top of the organization have most impact on strategy and policy, especially where that influences the decisions of elected members and the subsequent budget priorities that they decide on each financial year.

Figure 8.1 illustrates the structure of an imaginary council where libraries are under the remit of an education committee and in a department also consisting of museums and community education.

Figure 8.1 merely illustrates how responsibilities may work; the reality will differ from authority to authority, but the key point to understand is how the newer merged departments carry a massive range of service responsibilities with professionals from differing backgrounds all working under the same umbrella.

Increasingly within such structures it is often the case that the senior official in the hierarchy is not a professional with a library background. This need not have negative strategic consequences for the role of libraries in the hierarchy, but it does open up the possibility that this may be the case if the chief officer within the department does not understand the specific challenges and concerns of public libraries and the other members of the senior management team who do are not able to advocate for their service in an efficient way. As Midwinter and McVicar argued in their 1994 study, if a library service is 'absorbed into a large conglomerate department,

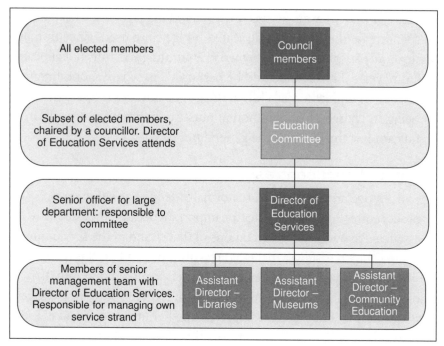

Figure 8.1 Mock-up governance model for library service under education committee

the important link between the chief librarian and the committee chairman may be broken' (Midwinter and McVicar, 1994, 74).

Budgets

Settlements to local government from central government take place each year, so there is no specific government allocation with regard to funding of public library services. It is then up to each individual local authority to allocate resources to each department under their remit. Once devolved to departments, budgets are allocated to specific areas of expenditure to enable proper use of finances. For instance it would not be good practice to draw on a staffing budget for books, or vice versa; thus allocations to specific spending blocks are an important aspect of good governance.

The financial year in a local authority runs from 1 April to 31 March, and it is important to be aware of this timetable for several reasons. Monies available to spend at the beginning of the financial year are likely to be larger than they are at the end. Equally a manager must keep on top of spending and ensure that allocated budgets are used, since in many contexts any surplus may be deemed over-funding and thus not allocated in future years if it is felt it could be best used elsewhere. Good financial management is an essential skill of the public library professional, then, as being in charge of public money puts the librarian in a position of significant responsibility to the general public.

Profit and cost centres

Specific budgetary allocations are normally defined as either cost centres or profit centres. These categories are important because they define what, in essence, the budgetary expectations of that strand of the service are.

A cost centre is a budget that is a direct draw on funding; it is not topped up through the year from sales of any other profit-making initiative. In public libraries this would account for a significant proportion of budgets, such as staffing, book purchasing, heating, lighting and the like. Profit centres on the other hand are budgets that directly add to the profits of the organization; they are added to throughout the financial year through sales or other money making initiatives. Some examples for public libraries might be sales of stationery or other items, rental of audio or video materials, or rental fees for library meeting rooms and the like. A fuller discussion of the importance of income generation in libraries can be found later in this chapter.

Capital expenditure

Capital expenditure is a crucial aspect of any organization's development. The term relates to expenditure that is strategically beyond the 12-month financial year in scope, such as new buildings, equipment and other infrastructure costs.

The most common aspects of capital expenditure for public libraries relate to the upkeep of the physical buildings or the construction of new ones. Since it is impossible to provide a library service without a building to house the collections, expenditure of this type is important, and normally very costly. It is important, then, that capital funds are separate from the funds needed to run the library service day to day.

Financing of capital projects can often necessitate the council obtaining funding from other sources, such as loans from financial institutions. In recent years the UK Government has urged public bodies of all kinds to adopt public-private partnerships (PPPs) under the Private Finance Initiative (PFI). PFI 'provides a way of funding major capital investments, without immediate recourse to the public purse. Private consortia, usually involving large construction firms, are contracted to design, build, and in some cases manage new projects. Contracts typically last for 30 years, during which time the building is leased by a public authority' (Department of Health, 2008).

Such schemes are not without their critics; they essentially mean that the new public buildings constructed under the arrangement are owned by a private company and leased back to the local authority.

There are several examples of PFI projects in the public libraries area, including the construction of new libraries in Bournemouth (Sibthorpe, 2001) as well as Lisburn in Northern Ireland, and two libraries in Newcastle upon Tyne.

Tendering

Another aspect of good governance in local authorities is the compulsion to issue tenders for any purchases that are over a spending threshold. The tender process is designed to ensure that large contracts are placed into the public domain where a bidding process can take place, in order that the process is open and transparent. This process can be either open, or restricted to several companies previously selected as offering high standards of service.

While upper limits on specific spending types vary slightly from one public organization to another, there is a consistent process for handling varying sizes of contract. From a service standpoint the key issue to remember is that procurement through a tendering process will add months to the timeline of obtaining the products or services concerned. For instance, if the procurement relates to the purchase of a new authority-wide library management system, it is likely to be a contract that would exceed the limit where it would have to be put out to tender within the European Union as well as in the UK (normally around £150,000). This is not merely an administrative concern, but a legal requirement under European law.

Sustainability of services

In the previous chapter we discussed the impact of ICTs on public libraries and the importance of sustainability. This is one of the key management challenges facing public libraries, since ICT-based services require significant investment over a renewable cycle of perhaps three or four years at a time. Research has suggested that the use of older ICT equipment inhibits the use of online services, and that users can become frustrated with equipment that does not allow the totality of uses of internet-based services (Schofield, McMenemy and Henderson, 2004). If users expect the computer to be able to deliver multimedia and allow memory-intensive software to run on it, then an older machine would appear slow and frustrating to use. This has a direct impact on service quality and user satisfaction.

Such large, regular infrastructure purchases need to be carefully managed; they are not only expensive but also potentially complex. Imagine a library service with 20 libraries, each containing five computers each with peripherals. It would not be wise for the computers in all libraries to be replaced in the same year, for several reasons:

■ cost
■ staff time
■ impact on service delivery.

Thus a sensible solution towards managing such purchases is to stagger the purchasing and installation. Crucially it means that planning for large infrastructure projects needs to be done over several years rather than one.

Income generation

It could be argued that the raising of revenue is not something that should concern a service that is offering a social educational function; however, the reality is that there is increasing pressure for public libraries to raise income as a means of augmenting their funding. This can take several forms:

- charges for audio and video lending
- charges for specialist services, e.g. business information, genealogy
- installation of retail outlets such as cafés
- book sales (either old discarded library material or new material or both)
- specific grants.

Audio and video rental

Libraries have charged for lending audio items for a long time, as these materials were generally deemed to be outwith the basic services users should expect. It was common for an annual fee to be charged for membership of the audio lending service in many public libraries, or an alternative was to charge a fee per item borrowed.

In the 1980s many public libraries also began to lend videos and latterly DVD movies, also for a fee. This was altogether a more controversial example of income generation than the lending of audio, since video rental was already lucrative business for the private sector and DVD rental remains a lucrative business to this day; in 2004 the DVD and video hire market was worth £460 million in the UK (Keynote, 2005).

Income from audiovisual stock in public libraries grew 146% in the ten-year period 1995 to 2005, although this reflects significant rises in the average purchase price of audio and video material (LISU, 2006, 19). Notwithstanding this, it is clear that income from these sources has risen exponentially in the period and has provided many libraries with a significant income to augment their public funding.

As Feather has discussed, the controversy in operating such services lies in the economies of scale that large, publicly funded organizations like public libraries can provide in direct competition to businesses providing the same service (Feather, 2008, 103). Take for example an independent DVD rental shop in a community. It may well have a public library in its potential catchment area, but the public library does not have the overheads the shop has because the public library is publicly funded. This may also mean the public library is open longer, can charge less in rentals and lend for longer, and can pay less for the DVDs it purchases because of the discounts on offer from suppliers due to the high volume of materials the local authority purchases from them. This all has the potential to put the rental shop at a major competitive disadvantage.

It is not the role of a publicly funded organization to operate in direct competition with local businesses and therefore income generation in this area will remain potentially controversial. Arguments in favour of such a service relate to the ability the public library has to offer a deeper range of rental options; rather than only blockbuster movies, the stock can also include less popular options or older movies that may not necessarily have large volume rental potential.

Charges for specialist services

Although most reference enquiries are likely to take a few minutes, some queries from users are so specialist or require so much time devoted to them that they become impractical for a public library to handle without charge. Common examples of such queries are in the areas of genealogical research and business information.

Researching of family history is a notoriously time-consuming endeavour. It is not uncommon for public libraries to receive letters from people around the world seeking to find out information about their ancestors and the origins of their family. People are often willing to pay for the information they require. Public libraries are not statutorily charged with providing such services, even though in many cases they are the location where genealogical information is stored and as such are likely to continue to receive such queries. In such a context it is common for libraries to charge for staff time to undertake searches for genealogical, family or local history information.

Equally businesses often require detailed searches to be done for information as diverse as marketing reports, patents and trade marks, and even lists of competitors. As a result specialist business information services with staff trained in commercial information seeking feature in several metropolitan public library services. These services often offer further tailored services at a charge for businesses, such as tender contract searches, and searches for other types of information that are either time consuming to undertake, or are needed quickly. A more detailed discussion of such services is provided in Chapter 5.

Installation of retail outlets such as cafés

The emergence in the 1990s of a new style of bookshop that allowed book buyers to partake of a coffee while browsing the books they may wish to purchase has greatly influenced many library authorities. This new model of bookshop consisted of attractive interior design, comfortable sofas and chairs, and normally a major coffee franchise such as Starbucks or Costa.

As bookshops have increasingly been seen as competitors but also a major inspiration in terms of ideas for public libraries, many librarians have adopted this style when developing services. The arguments for such a development relate this new bookshop model to a lifestyle choice, suggesting that adopting such a successful strand to the service will make public libraries more popular by extension, especially to a more youthful market that has embraced the new bookshop model.

Crucially the café also offers the opportunity to raise income, and the library coffee house is becoming increasingly popular for coffee franchises to house an outlet, as issues over location and infrastructure costs are already settled.

The influence of the bookshop model on emerging library design will be discussed in more detail in Chapter 11.

Book sales

Library-book sales are common across the UK and offer public libraries opportunities in several areas:

- positive public relations
- income generation
- ability to dispose of unwanted stock without throwing it out.

Thus library-book sales not only offer the opportunity to raise some much needed revenue, but can also be seen as a crucial aspect of stock turnover to allow unwanted items to find new homes.

Each library authority decides how to operate their sales, with some offering one large central sale a year, while others offer regular sales through their branch libraries. For example Durham County Council provides a programme of rotated timetabled sales throughout their branch network, offering the public a regular and accurate picture of which branch is currently holding a sale via their website (www.durham.gov.uk/libraries).

Direct marketing

A recent development in income generation is the scheme to place marketing materials within books as they are borrowed by users. The scheme offered 'advertisers 500,000 inserts in county libraries such as Essex, Dorset, Somerset and also Bromley, in Kent, and Leeds. It aims to cover the UK by the middle of 2008 with around 3m inserts being made available per month' (BBC News, 2007).

Cultural change in management and service delivery

Public library services have increasingly been called upon to find more efficient and creative ways of working, both in delivering services to users, and in administering them. Some recent initiatives are discussed below.

Partnership working

Public librarians are increasingly using the benefits of partnership working. This involves librarians working with other professionals outwith or within the local authority. Such partnerships can yield positive results and lead to enhanced service provision.

Some excellent examples of what has been dubbed joined up working are illustrated by Libraries and Information East Midlands (www.liem.org.uk), itself an organization devoted to advocating the use of partnership working within its geographic area. Projects undertaken by some of its member libraries include a digitization project, Picture the Past, using the images from the collections of four local public library services. By working together on the project the group was able to attract over £350,000 of Heritage Lottery Fund financing.

Another successful advocacy project for partnership working previously discussed in Chapter 6 was the Vital Link project, a reader development and basic skills initiative funded under the DCMS/Wolfson Public Libraries Challenge Fund. The project brought together nine public library services in England, spread across four regions, as well as The Reading Agency, National Literacy Trust, and the National Reading Campaign (Train, Usherwood and Brooks, 2002). The project evaluation concluded that public libraries had a major role to play in basic skills education, but it was crucial that cross-sectoral partnerships were used to do so. The National Literacy Trust maintains a Vital Link website (www.literacytrust.org.uk/vitallink/) offering resources and advice for library staff wishing to develop services for adult learners, confirming the role of outside agencies in supporting library staff.

Previously discussed examples of successful partnership working include the Real lifelong learning partnership in Glasgow, the SAILS initiative in Sunderland, as well as the Bookstart and Richard & Judy Reading Club campaigns, through The Reading Agency. In addition the PFI schemes discussed earlier in the chapter could be seen to involve a high level of partnership working.

Charitable status

In a new development in public library administration, the issue of charitable trust status has come onto the agenda. This has become a major discussion point after recent high profile transfers of public library and other council services to charitable trust status, the most recent example being that of Glasgow City Council.

The main arguments in favour of public libraries and other cultural services such as museums moving towards charitable trust status relate to taxation. A large metropolitan library service that manages many public library service points, in the case of Glasgow over 30, is liable to pay rates on all the buildings it manages. Since it is providing a public service this creates a massive dent in the finances. As a charitable trust it would receive 100% rates relief and save a significant sum. Other advantages include the ability to seek additional funding only available to charities, as well as exemption from taxes with relation to operating income, any surpluses generated through core activities, and any interest held on monies on deposit. The total savings for Glasgow were estimated at £9.7 million a year.

However, moving to charitable trust status is a major step, not without its opponents. Since a trust is run by a board of trustees rather than council officials, critics argue that its accountability is more questionable than that of a local authority department. There is also concern expressed about employee rights and benefits in the move from a local authority structure to one that is essentially a private company operating as a trust.

Given the immense financial benefits accrued by services that have made the move, it may well be that more public libraries in the UK follow the path towards charitable trust status in the future. The implications for service quality and impact on practice need to be carefully examined.

Leadership and management trends

The nature of leadership within the profession is as always a crucial aspect for the future. The profession operates thousands of service points under the banners of different employers, and it is difficult to arrive at a consistent model for providing public library services; thus leadership must not only be related to specific day to day library authority concerns, but also focus on wider professional concerns.

Challenges in succession management

As an ageing profession public librarianship has seen the issue of succession to leadership as being a pivotal debate in recent years. A major examination of the issue was conducted by a team at the University of Sheffield who undertook an analysis of the public library workforce, considering recruitment, retention and leadership issues within the sector (Usherwood et al., 2001).

The study reported a concern widely held within the public library profession that there was a lack of real leadership:

> The general consensus was that there was lack of leaders in the public
> library profession, and as yet no agreed and identified way in which a new
> generation of leaders might be fostered. There was agreement that we

need to address not just leadership at the top of the organisation, but leadership 'from the side', and right throughout the organisation.

(Usherwood et al., 2001, 91)

Crucially the study found little evidence of succession planning within the profession, so concerns raised would be unlikely to be addressed without action. A major suggestion within the report was that 'individual library services, and individual library authorities, will need to look beyond what is sufficient for their own authority, and consider what is necessary for the profession and its users as a whole' (Usherwood et al., 2001, 92). Within a local authority structure where professionals are employed to manage services for a specific user community this remains a challenge.

Society of Chief Librarians

A high level example of senior library officers meeting regularly to consider wider professional issues is the Society of Chief Librarians (www.goscl. com/). The society is made up of the heads of library services of England, Wales and Northern Ireland, and meets regularly to consider the wider issues facing all public libraries. It has a major role in advocacy and in helping form new legislation through presence on steering committees, but also in considering the impact of any new legislation adopted, as well as interfacing between stakeholders such as the MLA and others.

Public Library Authorities Conference

The major UK conference dealing with strategic issues in the wider public library profession is the Public Library Authorities Conference which rotates its venue and is normally led by a senior officer in the city or area hosting the conference.

The conference is aimed at senior library professionals and elected members, and presents speakers from this strategic background. As a gathering of library professionals and elected members it offers opportunities for advocacy and lobbying of councillors.

Emergence of managerialism

Managerialism is a recent management trend that has impacted on the public sector. This has led to subsequent concerns among some commentators about its potential impact on the public library profession.

Managerialism is a term for an approach to managing organizations that found prominence in the 1980s and 1990s. A key commentator on managerialism in the public sector defines it as: 'beliefs and practices at the core of which burns the seldom-tested assumption that better management will prove an effective solvent for a wide range of economic and social ills' (Pollitt, 1993, 1). At the heart of the managerialist approach lie 'doctrines [that] include more emphasis on "professional" management, the introduction of explicit measures of performance, a focus on outputs and results and an ever greater role played by "private sector styles" of management practice' (Adcroft and Willis, 2005, 387). In the late 1990s Clarke and Newman (1997) identified new managerialism as the most recent incarnation of the concept. In the public sector this has become known as new public management (NPM).

It has been suggested that NPM has 'blurred the distinction between public and private sectors where the government's role has become much more of a facilitator of services compared to the frontline provider of services' (Adcroft and Willis, 2005, 388). In the context of public libraries, in 1996 Usherwood suggested that 'it has been fashionable both in practice and in theory to promote a generic model of management, and to maintain that the differences between the public and private sectors were little more than cosmetic' (1996, 15). It could certainly be argued that the emphasis on commercial models for public libraries, and the enhanced importance of performance measurement regimes, to be discussed in Chapter 9, illustrate that managerialism is continuing to have an influence on public libraries and professional practice.

Conclusion

The public library system in the UK is part of a larger complex structure of services provided for local communities. It constantly competes with equally deserving services for finance and political attention, and thus advocacy from the profession is vital to reach the ears of elected members.

The public librarians who manage the services need to develop a thorough understanding of modern management and budgeting issues relating to their organization and how they can use new opportunities for the development of their services. In a bid to promote joined-up government, partnership and project-based working have become more common, with an emphasis on collegiality with other professions in order to deliver high quality services.

As changes to local authorities and how they are managed have evolved, opportunities for professional librarians to become involved in wider services beyond libraries have occurred, and professionals from other backgrounds have been able to become involved in the development of library services. This has advantages and potential disadvantages, as on the one hand while services can clearly benefit from external input, there is a danger that the professional values of librarianship may be diluted as a result. As an ongoing process it will be interesting to observe what impact these new ways of working have on service delivery and the professional status of public librarians. As commentators observed in 1994 when considering this issue, it will take more than a tacit belief that a good manager can manage any type of service regardless of their background: 'what Directors will require is not the glib rhetoric of the new managerialism, but the capacity to give sound professional advice based on detailed knowledge and understanding of the service' (Midwinter and McVicar, 1994, 74).

References

Adcroft, A. and Willis, R. (2005) The (Un)intended Outcome of Public Sector Performance Measurement, *International Journal of Public Sector Management*, **18** (5), 386–400.

BBC News (2007) Library Books Get Insert Adverts, http://news.bbc.co.uk/1/hi/uk/7075262.stm.

Clarke, J. and Newman, J. (1997) *The Managerial State: power, politics, and ideology in the remaking of social value*, Sage.

Department of Health (2008) *Private Finance Initiative*, www.dh.gov.uk/en/Procurementandproposals/ Publicprivatepartnership/Privatefinanceinitiative/index.htm.

Feather, J. (2008) *The Information Society: a study of continuity and change*, 5th edn, Facet Publishing.

Keynote (2005) *Video and DVD Retail and Hire – 2005*, Keynote Reports.

LISU (2006) *Annual Library Statistics 2006*, Library and Information Statistics Unit, Loughborough University, www.lboro.ac.uk/departments/ls/lisu/downloads/als06.pdf.

Midwinter, A. and McVicar, M. (1994) *The Size and Efficiency Debate: public library authorities in a time of change*, British Library R & D Report 6143, Library Association Publishing.

Pollitt, C. (1993) *Managerialism and the Public Services: cuts or cultural change in the 1990s?*, 2nd edn, Blackwell.

Schofield, F., McMenemy, D. and Henderson, K. (2004) People's Network Libraries: comparative case studies of old and new ICT learning centres, *Library Review*, **53** (3), 157-66.

Sibthorpe, R. (2001) A New Path to Follow – Private Finance Initiative, *Library Association Record*, **103** (4), April, 236-7.

Train, B., Usherwood, B. and Brooks, G. (2002) *The Vital Link: an evaluation report*, The University of Sheffield.

Usherwood, B. (1993) *Public Library Politics: the role of the elected member*, Library Association Publishing.

Usherwood, B. (1996) *Rediscovering Public Library Management*, Library Association Publishing.

Usherwood, B., Proctor, R., Bower, G., Coe, C., Cooper, J. and Stevens, T. (2001) *Recruit, Retain and Lead: the public library workforce study*, Centre for the Public Library and Information in Society, Department of Information Studies, University of Sheffield and Resource.

Chapter 9

Performance measurement and evaluation

Introduction

The varied nature of the services provided by public libraries we have discussed in the previous chapters can make it challenging to measure them effectively. It is straightforward enough to measure the number of books borrowed by a user, and this done across a population of tens of thousands will give statistical information that can be used to inform decision-making. Nevertheless book issues are only one small part of public library services, and statistics about book issues only give us a limited picture of how the library is impacting on its local community.

However, by attempting to measure all services provided by public libraries there is a 'danger that with the imposition of too many external quality and performance accreditation processes quality and performance measurement declines into box ticking, statistics generation, and form filling' (Rowley, 2005, 509). The challenge is creating a performance measurement regime that provides informative data while not wasting staff time and expense in excessive data gathering.

This chapter will discuss the types of performance data regularly collected for public libraries, outline the methods used to collect meaningful data, and consider the debates related to the potential of such data for informing best practice.

Performance measurement

First let us consider what is meant by the term performance measurement. Ultimately performance measurement is a management tool aimed at ensuring resources are well spent and that a service can guarantee a level of quality for all its stakeholders. Public libraries are paid for by all taxpayers and have the potential to be used by all taxpayers, thus everyone in society should have an interest in their good management. Librarians have a duty to their public to strive continually for best performance from their service, and performance measurement allows regular analysis to be undertaken to examine whether standards are being maintained.

Yet this is all obviously dependent on the performance measures that are adopted being fit for purpose. Performance measurement is concerned with *inputs* and *outputs*. From the point of view of public libraries, inputs are categories like cost involved in providing a service, and the number of staff hours involved in delivering a service. Outputs include services like number of enquiries undertaken, or number of books issued. Inputs involved in book issues include the selection, purchasing and processing of an item, cataloguing and classifying the item, and the time taken to place it on the shelf and issue it to a library user. All of these processes occur to provide one book issue, and all stages are essential components in providing that single statistic.

To be meaningful, performance measures are combined to create performance *indicators*. For instance, the output of the number of book issues is a relatively meaningless statistic unless one has a basis for understanding what the number of issues means. In a public library that served a tiny community 10,000 issues a month would be an indicator of far more success than the same number for a large central library. Therefore the combination of performance measures into performance indicators gives context to the data. Orr's (1973) criteria for a successful library performance indicator remain clear and concise:

- informativeness
- reproducibility
- validity
- appropriateness
- practicality
- comparability.

These six criteria include consideration of all pertinent issues. Is the indicator appropriate for the service being measured? Is it practical and straightforward to collect? Does it allow comparison between libraries in similar locations?

Modes of measurement

One of the challenges involved in measuring services is choosing the correct type of measurement for the particular aspect of the service being analysed. The measurement of performance can be broken down into two separate types of data gathering, namely *quantitative* and *qualitative*. Although quantitative data may well be useful for measuring many services, it may be inappropriate for others. As much as their services may be quantifiable in nature, public libraries mainly provide services that are social, educational and/or cultural in nature. Measuring numbers of visitors to a library, and numbers of issues, gives an indication of how widespread the use of the service is, but it does not give any sense of what patrons do with the services the public library provides. Therefore to ignore the social dynamic of the provision is a major mistake. Linley and Usherwood undertook a social audit of two public library services in 1998 and used qualitative techniques in their study. Their observation that 'we need rather more sophisticated approaches to assessing the value of public libraries than simply counting book issues' is an apt one and quite neatly reflects the complexities of why people use public libraries (Linley and Usherwood, 1998, 85). This is certainly the case if we are fully to understand the impact public library services have on users, their communities and wider society.

Returning again to book issues as an example, the patron may well be borrowing a book that does anything from piquing their interest in a new genre, to inspiring them to undertake a course, or visit a country or learn a new language. Equally the book issue may simply reflect one person's leisure activity for an evening or two. These are very personal end results from something that under quantitative measurement would be merely recorded as a single book issue. Ideally measurements of public library services would identify the impact services are having on the lives and experiences of library patrons; this could then be used to build up a larger picture of the impact the library is having on its community. The difficulty is in measuring these impacts economically and effectively. For instance it is a straightforward task to measure book issues, since it is an automated process normally undertaken by the library management system which produces statistics when required.

Ultimately to determine the impact book issues have on patrons would involve interviewing or surveying all of them. Obviously this would be neither possible nor practical, therefore interviewing or surveying a selective sample of users would be one way of using qualitative methods in evaluating services. This can sometimes be undertaken by using a focus group, a representative sample of users that meets regularly to answer questions related to their use of the service. Focus groups can be enormously valuable routes to gathering qualitative data on service usage. They can also be, and often are, undertaken via a large-scale survey programme aimed at interviewing as many patrons in an allotted period of time as is practicable. In the UK the use of the PLUS survey has offered public libraries the opportunity to learn more about how their services are perceived by users. PLUS surveys will be discussed later in the chapter.

Measurement of public library services

Performance measurement for public libraries could be seen as being a professional concern across the globe given that public libraries exist in all corners of the planet. Realistically the performance indicators used to measure the effectiveness of public libraries vary depending on the country.

International examples

The International Federation of Library Associations (IFLA) publishes a suggested list of performance indicators which it suggests can be used for measuring public library services. These are:

■ *Usage indicators*
  - loans per capita
  - total library visits per capita
  - membership as a percentage of the population
  - loans per item - turnover of resources
  - reference enquiries per capita
  - loans per opening hour
■ *Resource indicators*
  - total book stock per capita
  - provision of terminals or personal computers per capita
  - provision of OPACs per capita
■ *Human resource indicators*
  - ratio of full-time equivalent staff to population
  - ratio of full-time equivalent staff to library use
■ *Qualitative indicators*
  - user satisfaction surveys
■ *Cost indicators*
  - unit costs for functions, services and activities
  - staff costs per functions, e.g. books processed, programmes
  - total costs per capita, per member, per visitor, per service point, etc.

(IFLA, 2000)

IFLA's suggested indicators are quite broad, although it is interesting to see qualitative indicators consisting solely of user satisfaction surveys. However, this allows for a large element of freedom on the part of the individual public library service to measure specific parts of the service qualitatively and, as previously seen, in the UK the PLUS series of surveys allow valuable feedback to be gathered in this way.

In the USA an annual publication each September by the National Center for Education Statistics lists a range of statistics about American public libraries. Many of the statistics published are similar to those recommended by IFLA. The 27 sets of tables include such diverse statistics as:

■ number of full-time equivalent staff by position (including professional librarians)

- number of public use internet terminals
- total per capita operating revenue of public libraries
- number and square footage of libraries.

(National Center for Education Statistics, 2005)

This is a weighty publication and includes data for every US state, presented side by side.

Performance indicators in UK libraries

The performance measurement regime for public libraries in the UK reflects the separation of responsibility for public services for each of the home countries since the devolution programme of the late 1990s.

A key policy development in the evaluation of public services in the UK was the introduction of the Best Value regime by the Labour Government shortly after it took power in 1997. The Best Value regime was designed to be more reflective and not be solely based around quantitative measurement. Each service provider was charged with asking questions of the service based around four categories, which became labelled as the four Cs:

- *Challenge*: is the service you are providing actually necessary? To the levels you are delivering it?
- *Compare*: how is your performance against other library services?
- *Consult*: ensure that all stakeholders have their opinion on the service sought.
- *Compete*: honestly appraise whether another organization could be better at providing your service than you are.

Chartered Institute of Public Finance and Accountancy

All public libraries in the UK must make an annual submission to the Chartered Institute of Public Finance and Accountancy (CIPFA). The submissions consist of detailed spreadsheets, downloaded from the CIPFA website and completed by a senior officer in each public library service. The questions answered consist of a series of performance related matters, such as issues in different categories, numbers of staff, numbers of computers, time taken to satisfy requests and so on. Financial data related to expenditure on categories of stock is also included, as well as measurement of enquiries not face to face, such as by telephone and e-mail.

Public Library User Surveys

CIPFA also administers the Public Library User Surveys (PLUS), which focus on more qualitative information in terms of user satisfaction levels. The surveys are split into four sections for respondents to answer:

1   your activity today,
2   the outcome of your visit,
3   how you rate the services provided, and, finally,
4   about you.

(IPF, 2008)

As can be seen the sections focus on specific library usage on the day the user was visiting, the satisfaction they had in their visit on that day, general satisfaction about the library service, and demographic information on them as an individual.

Variations of the PLUS model include a survey for children, and one designed to elicit wider community feedback, which can be undertaken as a postal survey, thus reaching users and non-users. Another recently developed is ePLUS, which allows public libraries to ascertain user satisfaction levels with the ICT services provided.

A changing landscape

The greatest number of changes in how the performance of public libraries has been measured has been seen in England in the period since 1997. Figure 9.1 illustrates the changes seen between 1998 and 2009.

1998	• Annual library plans • *Framed under Best Value regime*
2001	• Public Library Standards • *26 in total*
2002	• Public library position statements (*replacing annual library plans*)
2004	• Public Library Service Standards (10) • *Replaced public library position statements and the original Public Library Standards*
2009	• Comprehensive area assessments

Figure 9.1 Ways of measuring public library
performance 1998–2009

Annual library plans

Annual library plans (ALPs) were introduced in 1998 and sought to ensure that library authorities were responsive to performance on short and long-term goals. Plans were produced over a three-year rolling programme with Part A providing a general background to the authority and library service and produced every three years and Part B providing a performance appraisal and development plan, produced annually.

Public Library Standards

In 2001 the Department for Culture, Media and Sport produced the report *Comprehensive, Efficient and Modern Public Libraries*, aimed at recommending a set of performance measures for the modern library service (DCMS, 2001). This document introduced 26 standards that public libraries had to respond to, and made it compulsory for ALPs to contain:

■ Local targets for services to the following groups:
  — children
  — socially excluded people
  — ethnic minority communities
  — people with disabilities

■ An explanation of how regional and cross-border patterns of library use affect services (especially in London), and how this is reflected in the way services are planned and coordinated in co-operation with other library authorities.

(DCMS, 2001, 8)

Public library position statements

Public library position statements were introduced in 2002 to replace ALPs. The statement was required to identify all the library services provided by the local authority and to discuss the strengths, weaknesses and performance of each. These statements were in turn replaced in 2004 with ten newly streamlined Public Library Service Standards, also replacing the original 26 Public Library Standards introduced in 2001. In 2009 these standards will be replaced by comprehensive area assessments.

Comprehensive area assessments

The Audit Commission describes a comprehensive area assessment (CAA) as follows:

■ It is about people and places.
■ It will give people a snapshot of life in their local area each year.
■ It will help local services improve quality of life in their area.
■ It will help people understand if they are getting value for money from their local services.

(Audit Commission, 2008)

Public library services will need to show evidence of how CAAs are helping to achieve key priority targets. The focus will be based on outcomes and on how the service is improving the local community. The new CAAs reflect an ongoing culture of measurement that is moving towards self-assessment as a means of measuring service impact.

Virtual users

An increasing challenge facing libraries across the sectors is the conflict inherent in concentrating on the number of people who visit library buildings as opposed to those who visit the library virtually. As more and more services are provided digitally, more emphasis needs to be placed on the visitor to the library website as a valid service user. Another challenge the virtual library model brings is the increasing use of library services by people outside the geographical area funded. This is especially important with regard to public library services, since funding is normally provided for citizens of a specific geographic locale. If increasing use is made of the service by patrons from outside the geographic area served, questions may begin to be asked about providing value for money and who exactly is paying for the service. This is a political hot potato that public libraries have grappled with in the physical world, and can only be exacerbated in the virtual world.

Measurement of Scottish public libraries

Performance indicators for Scottish public libraries are published annually as part of the Cultural and Community Services indicators (Audit Scotland, 2007) and based around additions to stock, usage of libraries, and numbers of users of learning centres and ICT facilities. These statistics are relatively straightforward and are published as league tables, highlighting those authorities that are in the top 10 of each category and which have improved year on year.

Towards qualitative measurement in Scotland

The first Public Library Improvement Matrix (PLIM) was created after a two-year project funded by the British Library Research and Innovation Centre and conducted by researchers at the universities of Loughborough and Sheffield. The PLIM provided library managers with a toolkit consisting of a self-assessment questionnaire, a management and improvement matrix and a pro-forma to aid with improvements, communication and future service objectives. Although a significant qualitative alternative to static quantitative evaluation tools, PLIM required ongoing monitoring and improvements to evolve with changes in politics and user demands (Jones, Kinnell and Usherwood, 2000, 134-5).

Seven years after the development of the Public Library Improvement Matrix the Scottish Executive and the Scottish Library and Information Council produced its own self-assessment toolkit, the Public Library Quality Improvement Matrix (SLIC, 2007). This toolkit provided 'a robust method for defining standards, developing evaluation criteria and a planning tool to ensure services meet public demand' (SLIC, 2007, 6). Seven quality indicators (QIs) were defined as a benchmark for public libraries to measure their success against:

1   Access to information
2   Community and personal participation
3   Meeting readers' needs
4   Learners' experiences
5   Ethos and values
6   Organisation and use of resources and space
7   Leadership.

(SLIC, 2007)

The matrix is supported by a set of guidelines for each QI, which includes a range of themes and examples to help library managers make judgements and identify best practice. Public library authorities must evaluate themselves on a success scale between 1 and 6, where 1 equals 'unsatisfactory' and 6 equals 'excellent'. Service managers are also encouraged to conduct stakeholder consultations and observations before defining outcomes.

Measuring economic value

This brings us neatly to the issue of value for money and public library services. A recent development in assessing the impact of public libraries has seen a movement to try to ascertain the economic value they provide. Quantitative measurement measures output and qualitative measurement attempts to measure economic impacts, which can be loosely defined as value for money.

Contingent valuation

Another such system is called contingent valuation, and aims to survey not only users, but also non-users. Therefore, it makes sense to assess library performance in terms of economic value. Aabø and Audunsen define contingent valuation as a method that 'draws upon economic theory and the methods of survey research to elicit directly from citizens the value they place upon goods not traded in private markets' (Aabø and Audunsen, 2002).

Contingent valuation uses rational choice theory in which people are held to calculate the likely costs and benefits of any action before deciding what to do. In rational choice theory, individuals are seen as motivated by the wants or goals that express their 'preferences'. Rational choice theory holds that individuals must anticipate the outcomes of alternative courses of action and calculate that which will be best for them. The theory is that rational individuals choose the alternative that is likely to give them the greatest satisfaction. Contingent valuation works through constructing a market by an interview survey of its potential players (Aabø and Audunsen, 2002) using:

- a scenario or description of the hypothetical or real policy or programme the respondent is being asked to value or vote on
- a mechanism for eliciting value or a choice from the respondent
- information on the respondent's socioeconomic characteristics, attitude and behaviour towards the good to be valued, and whether the respondent understood and believed the scenario and took the hypothetical decision-making seriously.

The contingent valuation of the service can be calculated by comparing the perceived return on the service to the actual costs of the service and the costs users incurred accessing the service. Contingent valuation is also potentially good at measuring non-use values, something that traditional quantitative and qualitative measures do not do – for example, a person who does not go to the public library will have little opinion on the quality of its reference services. However, they may still place value on the public library reference service in terms of its worth to society. Contingent valuation generates quantitative results, which can then be interpreted in a qualitative manner – understanding users' attitudes towards the library, for example what services they value, rather than understanding user behaviour and actions alone, that is how many books are borrowed.

The method has already been applied to public library services in several countries. There have been three major studies. St Louis Public Libraries (1999) surveyed branches separately and found returns on US$1 were US$1.30–2.70 in Birmingham Public Library to US$10 or more in Phoenix Public Library. Differences in return were also found for the same service at different locations. Griffiths, King and Lynch (2004) looked at investment in Florida State Libraries and found that US$6.84 was returned for every US$1 spent. Barron et al. (2005) looked at South Carolina State Libraries and found a direct return on investment of US$ 4.48 for every US$1 spent on public libraries. Bolton Metropolitan Borough Council and MLA North West (2005) found a low return of £1.60 for every £1 spent. In comparison, a recent use of the methodology at the British Library suggested that for every £1 spent on the service, a return of £4 is generated (Pung, Clarke and Patten, 2004). In recent years Aabø (2005) has attempted to apply the method to the Norwegian public library service as a whole.

As Missingham (2005) observes there are issues in using numerical values as a measure of success – how comparable are they and is there a potential to find a benchmark, what causes variations in results and what contextual and external factors might affect a contingent valuation study? To a large extent these issues relate back to the core proposition of contingent valuation, that people can make rational economic judgements about hitherto 'unvalued' services.

The consequences of performance measurement

The reality is that public libraries will continue to have to justify their existence to taxpayers and government, both local and central. A school of thought could be posited that since they are essentially good things to have, public libraries should not be strictly measured, but this does not reflect reality. The fact is that if a public library is seen to be under-used then its future may be in jeopardy. Therefore embracing a robust regime for performance measurement is crucial for all public libraries. This regime must be more than a mere league table of libraries and needs to take into account the diversity of services offered by the modern public library. It must place equal emphasis on qualitative data gathering in order that we better understand what library patrons are using their service for and what impact this has on their life.

League table syndrome?

In some of the official publications we have discussed in this chapter we have seen how quantitative measurement can result in a league table approach. This is unhealthy for a service that is designed to be socially inclusive because ironically the communities with the greatest need for the types of services provided by public libraries may be the very communities who use their services the least. This needs to be remembered when mulling over statistical data, and certainly when decisions are made related to potential library closures as a result of perceived under-performance.

New services and innovation

The performance measurement regime in public libraries also needs to be reflective enough to take into consideration potential new services. If public libraries are measured on the same set of statistics year in and year out, and the focus of managers is constantly on ensuring that improving these statistics is the primary goal of the organization, it follows that innovation in new service provision can become a casualty. This is counterproductive for a modern service that aims to meet the needs of users.

It is quite clear that, given the wide variety and complexity of the services provided by the public libraries in today's world, it may be useful to set measurement criteria for each strand of service provided by public libraries and appropriate methods for data collection, which may comprise both qualitative and quantitative methods. However, evaluating specific service strands is not the same thing as evaluating the entire service. Moreover, since public libraries' service delivery and impact depends on the socio-economic infrastructure of their locality, it is important to attach appropriate conditions or parameters to performance criteria for each strand. Comparing an area with a high level of economic need with one that is affluent is potentially meaningless, yet the league table method does just that. Ensuring that performance measurement is representative and fair is perhaps the crucial goal for successful measurement.

Defining value

Movement to assessing economic value using methods like contingent valuation also has its dangers. If we begin to see public libraries from the point of view of how much economic value they add to a community, the potential for that consideration to become uppermost in the minds of managers and stakeholders when measuring services becomes a real danger. If it is found, for instance, that a public library adds less in economic value than is spent on it, does this negate the worth of the services provided? It is a crucial question to consider as this system of measuring value becomes more prominent.

Conclusion

The recent moves we are seeing towards a rethinking on public library evaluation are an interesting development. There is an irrefutable logic in seeking to measure how successful public libraries are for their communities, yet such endeavours have to yield meaningful results if they are to help influence the service development of public libraries for the better.

As services move towards more qualitative methods of evaluation, and the emphasis on self-assessment grows, the opportunities for public librarians to shape performance measurement regimes in a more positive way become greater. Good professionals concern themselves with quality of service, but this must be built around meaningful evaluation of services in order that the data gathered can be used to improve services. Thus a refocusing away from inputs and outputs to actual tangible outcomes is a move forward in terms of a holistic understanding of service effectiveness.

An ever-evolving standards regime poses logistical challenges for public servants who seek to implement one system and work towards achieving the goals it sets out, only to have the system changed on them again and again. Unfortunately this is the nature of professional practice in a political culture, but the emphasis on ensuring a quality service for library users should be at the forefront of all systems of measurement.

References

Aabø, S. (2005) *The Value of Public Libraries*, paper presented at the World Library and Information Congress, Oslo, Norway, www.ifla.org/IV/ifla71/papers/119e-Aabo.pdf.

Aabø, S. and Audunsen, R. (2002) Rational Choice and Valuation of Public Libraries: can economic models for evaluating non-market goods be applied to public libraries?, *Journal of Library and Information Science*, **34** (1), 5–16.

Audit Commission (2008) *What is Comprehensive Area Assessment (CAA)?*, www.audit-commission.gov.uk/caa/.

Audit Scotland (2007) *Cultural and Community Services*, www.audit-scotland.gov.uk/performance/docs/2007/service/compCComS07.pdf.

Barron, D. D. et al. (2005) *The Economic Impact of Public Libraries in South Carolina*, School of Library and Information Science, University of South Carolina, www.libsci.sc.edu/SCEIS/impact_brochure.pdf.

Bolton Metropolitan Borough Council and MLA North West (2005) *Bolton's Museum, Library and Archive Services: an economic evaluation*, http://research.mla.gov.uk/evidence/documents/bolton_main.pdf.

DCMS (2001) *Comprehensive, Efficient and Modern Public Libraries: standards and assessment*, Department for Culture, Media and Sport, www.culture.gov.uk/PDF/libraries_pls_assess.pdf.

Griffiths, J. M., King, D. W. and Lynch, T. (2004) *Taxpayer Return on Investment in Florida Public Libraries: summary report*, http://dlis.dos.state.fl.us/bld/roi/pdfs/ROISummaryReport.pdf.

IFLA (2000) *Revision of IFLA's Guidelines for Public Libraries*, www.ifla.org/VII/s8/proj/gpl.htm#2.

IPF (2008) PLUS - Public Library User Surveys,
    www.ipfmarketresearch.net/culture/plus/default.asp.

Jones, K., Kinnell, M. and Usherwood, B. (2000) The Development of
    Self-Assessment Tool-Kits for the Library and Information Sector,
    Journal of Documentation, **52** (2), 120-35.

Linley, R. and Usherwood, B. (1998) *New Measures for the New Library:
    a social audit of public libraries*, British Library Research &
    Innovation Centre Report 89, Centre for the Public Library and
    Information in Society.

Missingham, R. (2005) Libraries and Economic Value: a review of
    recent studies, *Performance Management and Metrics*, **6** (3),
    142-58.

National Center for Education Statistics (2005) *Public Libraries in the
    United States: fiscal year 2003*,
    http://nces.ed.gov/surveys/libraries.

Orr, R. H. (1973) Measuring the Goodness of Library Services: a
    general framework for considering quantitative measures, *Journal
    of Documentation*, **29**, 315-32.

Pung, C., Clarke, A. and Patten, L. (2004) Measuring the Economic
    Impact of the British Library, *New Review of Academic
    Librarianship*, **10** (1), April, 79-102.

Roberts, S. and Rowley, J. (2004) *Managing Information Services*, Facet
    Publishing.

Rowley, J. (2005) Making Sense of the Quality Maze: perspectives for
    public and academic libraries, *Library Management*, **26** (8/9),
    508-18.

SLIC (2007) *Building on Success: a public library quality improvement
    matrix for Scotland*, Scottish Library and Information Council and
    Scottish Executive.

St Louis Public Libraries (1999) *Using Your Library: public library
    benefits valuation study, St Louis Public Library*,
    www.slpl.lib.mo.us/using/valuationtoc.htm.

Chapter 10

Professional and staffing issues

Introduction

One of the most vital aspects of any service are the people who plan and deliver it; in public library terms the staff are the key asset in delivering the service to the library user. Public libraries are made up of teams of staff who deliver the diverse range of services previously discussed in Chapters 3 to 6.

This chapter will discuss the nature of the skills required in public library staff, the professional networks that exist to sustain them, and other issues that impact on staff well-being and development.

The local authority staffing structure

As discussed in Chapter 8, public libraries in the UK are part of local authority structure and staff fit within a broad salary and grading structure that reflects their qualifications and experience. Staff roles are normally divided between professional and paraprofessional responsibilities.

Professional and paraprofessional

As discussed, functions within public libraries are shared between professional and paraprofessional staff. The nature of which duties should be undertaken by each is sometimes a matter of debate and controversy, as will be discussed further below, and in some library authorities the distinction between duties carried out is blurring.

Professional duties are normally those that require knowledge of librarianship, for instance leading in reader development activities for children or adults, as well as making and maintaining professional links across the service, and taking responsibility for a service-wide function such as young people's or adult services, or an inclusion remit. Paraprofessional duties are designed to support these activities and will require more direct involvement with the general public, some basic enquiry and reference work, and perhaps undertaking initiatives in the library that have been planned by the professional staff, such as reading activities, facilitating reading groups, and the like.

As more library authorities have moved from the old model of having a librarian based in and responsible for each library branch, increasingly paraprofessional staff are charged with higher levels of responsibility, such as holding keys for the building, managing a staff team, monitoring revenues, and maintaining sickness and absence records for the branch they manage. These roles are normally for senior library assistants and offer promotion opportunities for paraprofessional staff.

The most up to date statistics produced from the Library and Information Statistics Unit (LISU) suggest that the number of professional public library posts has fallen significantly across the UK. While the total number of posts per 10,000 population has fallen 5% over the period 1995–2005, professional library posts have fallen by 15% in the same period (Creaser, Maynard and White, 2006, 21).

Professional issues

Public librarianship is a subset of librarianship, a profession that encompasses many sectors, including academic, school, health, law and other library types. Professions are normally categorized as being distinct from occupations for several reasons:

- All members must be trained in a body of knowledge.
- Normally members require a university education to achieve this.
- There is a professional body that accredits the above.

■ There is an ethical code administered by the professional body adhered to by all members.

From this rubric public librarianship clearly can be described as a profession, as most professional posts in public libraries in the UK require Chartered Membership of the relevant professional body, the Chartered Institute of Library and Information Professionals (CILIP).

Chartered Institute of Library and Information Professionals

The professional body that represents librarians from all sectors in the UK is CILIP, following the merger between the former Library Association and the Institute of Information Scientists.

CILIP has several categories of Membership, which encompass professional staff, paraprofessional staff and organizations. These are the categories of relevance to those working within the public library sector in the UK:

■ *Affiliated Membership*: open to anyone working in a post within a library or information service that does not require professional qualifications – typically those working as information or library assistants. Affiliated Members can apply for our new Certification qualification which will entitle them to use the letters ACLIP after their name.

■ *Student Membership*: open to people in full or part-time education on an accredited course in library and information science in the UK, and graduate trainees on pre-postgraduate experience.

■ *Associate Membership*: to be eligible for Associate Membership you need to have an information or library qualification accredited by CILIP, or another academic qualification coupled with a period of work experience at a professional level. Associate Members are eligible to apply for Chartered Membership.

■ *Chartered Membership (MCLIP)*: to become a Chartered Member you need to successfully complete a portfolio of professional development, which evidences your experience and skills. Chartered Membership is considered the 'gold standard' for library and information professionals.

■ *Chartered Fellowship (FCLIP)*: to become a Chartered Fellow you need to demonstrate that as a Chartered Member you have continued your professional development for a period of time (usually at least 6 years) and that you have made a significant contribution to all or part of the profession.

■ *Honorary Fellowship (Hon FCLIP)*: is awarded by CILIP Council to individuals who have rendered distinguished service in promoting the objects of the Institute. Nominations may be made by Members, Branches, Groups, or committees and sub committees of Council.

■ *Institutions and organizations*: CILIP has two categories of Membership for organizations. Library and information services in the UK and overseas can join CILIP as Institutional Members. Other organizations such as library or information suppliers should join the Suppliers network, where we have created a special package of benefits tailored to their needs.

(www.cilip.org.uk/membership/faqs/membershipfaq1.htm)

CILIP qualifications

The Membership types of ACLIP, MCLIP and FCLIP are formal categories that are achieved through the completion of a designated mix of qualifications and experience.

Professional posts within public libraries are commonly limited to candidates with a degree level qualification in library and information studies or a variation thereof, and it is also common to see Chartership stated as a requirement. For some posts MCLIP status is acceptable without a degree in the subject and this may well become more common with the introduction of the recently developed ACLIP qualification, which offers a route to MCLIP status for those without a degree in library studies.

The CILIP mentoring programme runs to aid Members who wish to seek a route to one of the qualifications through providing a list of mentors in each region that prospective candidates can contact to agree a mentoring arrangement. Although not compulsory for the ACLIP route, it remains a useful and viable approach to achieving the qualification.

CILIP special interest groups

Members of CILIP can join two special interest groups (SIGs) for areas of practice of interest or direct relevance to the Members, and subsequent groups can be joined for a fee.

Each SIG is governed by regulations set down by CILIP and is normally run by a committee drawn from its Membership body. Many run conferences and continuing professional development events, and publish their own journals or newsletters. A list of groups that may be of interest to staff working in the public library sector is given below, with an overview of their activities:

- *Affiliated Members of CILIP*: for supporting Affiliated Members of CILIP and those seeking to gain this category of Membership.
- *Branch and Mobile Libraries*: to support staff working in smaller branch libraries and particularly mobile libraries. Organizes a regular conference with the Public Libraries Group.
- *Career development*: a group aimed at new entrants to the profession, its work is closely involved with preparing new entrants to the MCLIP process.
- *Cataloguing and Indexing*: a group aimed at those working in the classification and cataloguing field or those interested in the topic.
- *Community Services*: aims to promote the use of libraries to the wider community to help aid in community cohesion. A popular group for public librarians given its socially inclusive mission.
- *Diversity Group*: aims to unite Members engaged with or interested in diversity issues related to library and information services. The group defines diversity as 'issues of race, religion, culture, ethnicity, class, gender, sexuality, age, disability – and other factors that result in discrimination and inequality'.

■ *Information Services*: although not uniquely aimed at public libraries, the group draws many Members from the sector and publishes important guides of direct interest such as *Guidelines for Reference and Information Services in Public Libraries* (ISG, 1999) and *Basic Reference Resources for the Public Library* (Dixon et al., 2005).

■ *Library and Information History*: interested in the history of libraries and librarianship. Produces newsletters and a scholarly journal, *Library History*. The group studies public library history as a discipline of scholarship and has encouraged several studies on the topic.

■ *Library and Information Research*: cross-sectoral group that promotes the link between research and practice in librarianship. Offers an annual research award for practitioners to undertake research.

■ *Local Studies*: aimed directly at public librarians working with local history materials. Develops standards and offers meetings and workshops aimed at the community, as well as lobbying on the topic. Key publication is *The Local Studies Librarian*.

■ *Multimedia Information & Technology*: aimed at Members interested in multimedia and technology issues. Useful for public librarians involved in People's Network services or other aspects of ICT development.

■ *Patent and Trademark Group*: of interest to those public librarians who may be working in a business information role within their library authority.

■ *Personnel, Training and Education*: cross-sectoral group focused around training issues and organizing appropriate training opportunities for library staff. Also organizes mentor support for the CILIP mentoring programme.

■ *Public Libraries Group*: the main group for CILIP Members engaged in work in the public library sector. Organizes two regular conferences, one with the Branch Mobiles Group, and the Public Library Authorities Conference. Key publication is *Public Libraries Journal*.

■ *Publicity and Public Relations*: promotes the importance of high quality publicity and public relations for libraries. Organizes an annual conference, and offers awards for libraries that have produced high quality publicity campaigns.

■ *Rare Books and Special Collections Group*: a cross-sectoral group aimed at librarians working with rare materials and special collections. It 'promotes the study and exploitation of rare books, encourages awareness of preservation, conservation and digitization issues, and fosters training opportunities related to the maintenance, display and use of collections'.

■ *Youth Libraries Group*: a vital group for public library staff engaged in work with children and developing children's services. It targets for Membership 'librarians, information professionals and all those working with or interested in children's and young people's books, reading development, the promotion of libraries and reading for pleasure'. Organizes an annual conference, a journal, *Youth Libraries Review*, and has been instrumental in producing standards documents in the area, such as *Start With the Child* and *A Safe Place for Children* (discussed in Chapter 4).

CILIP's Body of Professional Knowledge

The Body of Professional Knowledge that CILIP uses to accredit all courses in information and library studies throughout the UK is represented by the schema illustrated in Figure 10.1.

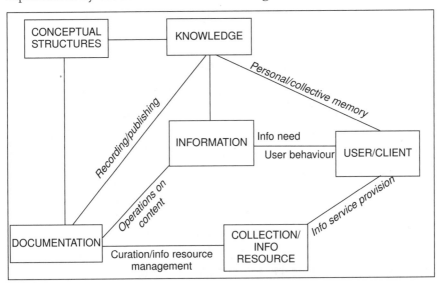

Figure 10.1 CILIP's Body of Professional Knowledge
(Source: www.cilip.org.uk/qualificationschartership/bpk)

Each rectangle represents an important aspect of professional competency. The core concept is knowledge, which is used in this context to represent the collected memory of society. *Knowledge* is handled using *conceptual structures* such as classification schemes, which are used in libraries and archives (*documentation*) as part of the wider publishing and information cycle. *Information* is communicated to users based on their expressed needs and wants. The materials are handled using *collection/information resource management*, which allows for everything from selection and acquisitions through to providing an information service to the user.

The Body of Professional Knowledge also encompasses an ethical framework, which all CILIP Members are required to be aware of and adhere to.

Ethical issues

In Chapter 3 we touched on the values of librarianship as seen through the eyes of two writers on the topic, Ranganathan and Gorman, as well as some of the ethical issues public librarians may be faced with in delivering services to library users. In a more formal capacity public librarians who are Members of CILIP are charged with adhering to a Code of Professional Practice, which governs the standards of their professional behaviour.

CILIP Code of Professional Practice

The ethical principles laid down by CILIP are encompassed in two important documents, the statement Ethical Principles for Library and Information Professionals and the Code of Professional Practice. The ethical principles are a list of 12 values, such as 'Concern for the public good' and 'Concern for the good reputation of the information profession'. These principles also include:

- impartiality, and avoidance of inappropriate bias, in acquiring and evaluating information and in mediating it to other information users
- respect for confidentiality and privacy in dealing with information users
- concern for the conservation and preservation of our information heritage in all formats

- respect for, and understanding of, the integrity of information items and for the intellectual effort of those who created them
- commitment to maintaining and improving personal professional knowledge, skills and competences.

The set of ethical principles, then, stand as a core set of values that can be clearly seen to be of relevance and importance to public libraries. Within the Code of Professional Practice itself more detail is provided about specific responsibilities that the librarian has to themselves and society. The Code of Professional Practice has sections on:

- personal responsibilities
- responsibilities to information and its users
- responsibilities to colleagues and the information community
- responsibilities to society
- responsibilities as employees.

The section 'Personal Responsibilities' emphasizes professional competency and professional development, although it also calls on Members not to claim any expertise in an area they are not familiar with. In 'Responsibilities to Information and its Users' the code discusses ensuring that the user is aware of the wide range of services on offer, and that access to information is as straightforward as possible. Within this theme is also stressed the need to be impartial in selection of resources, the need to treat user queries with confidentiality, and to ensure that any competing needs of information users are fairly dealt with. There is an emphasis on the balancing act of protecting the user's right to access versus the right of the creator of a work to legal and moral protection from abuse of their work. This section concludes with a reminder of the librarian's role to preserve the knowledge of mankind for future generations. It addresses copyright and other legal obligations that the library has a role in protecting.

'Responsibilities to Colleagues and the Information Community' promotes the notion of ethical behaviour towards colleagues, highlighting the need to encourage the development of the skills of co-workers and employees. Interestingly, within this set of values aimed at promoting best practice in the service and in colleagues is a call to 'report significant breaches of this Code to the appropriate authorities'.

The section 'Responsibilities to Society' emphasizes the role of the librarian in promoting equitable access to information, and in working to ensure that the balance between access and protection of information resources is met. This section also calls on Members to ensure that the ethical code is promoted to colleagues and society as a whole.

'Responsibilities as Employees' discusses the need for Members to become engaged with the mission of the entire organization, not just the library or information service. This is an important point for the public librarian who is an employee of a local authority rather than a library in isolation. The need to ensure the organization is operating ethically is also stressed, with a call to 'bring to the attention of their employer any concerns they may have concerning the ethics or legality of specific decisions, actions or behaviour at work'.

Professional vs paraprofessional

As mentioned above, debates about which duties are carried out by different designations of staff occur frequently. Ongoing in library services, this debate also occupies wider professional discourse, and in recent years has been a prominent and controversial topic of interest within the professional body and the wider public library service.

Public Library Authorities Conference 2007 debate

A debate at the 2007 Public Library Authorities Conference was based around the heading: 'Deprofessionalisation and the 21st century library'. The proposal for the debate was 'this house believes that holding on to the requirements for library qualifications and Chartership stands in the way of public libraries making the transformational change needed for a modern service'.

Clearly a controversial topic, there was much debate afterwards in the professional press, exacerbated by the fact that the motion was passed at the conference. Those in favour suggested that modern public libraries were less in need of traditional library skills and more in need of people with good interpersonal and customer service experience. Those who opposed it raised the spectre of deprofessionalization as a major concern for the longevity of the public library profession and the quality of the service on offer.

The Conway Report

CILIP commissioned a report into the issue of professional standards of service as a direct result of the ongoing debate, and it was published in May 2008. The report considered what could be deemed professional standards of service, and examined more closely several library authorities that it was felt were in danger of damaging their standards through paths towards deprofessionalization.

Conway attempted to define four key areas where public libraries should be deemed to operate professionally under their legal obligations:

- A satisfying experience for the user visiting the library, in terms of environment, procedures, and stock and services, provided by courteous, helpful and knowledgeable staff.
- A developed casework approach relating to individual needs, where the user benefits from an officer's professional judgement. This could cover, for example, giving information and advice, reading development, learning opportunities both formal and informal, and specialist subject support in local studies, business and commerce, health, etc.
- Determining local operational priorities for a library or group of libraries and developing local partnerships with other organisations, taking into account the profile of the community and its needs. This would cover stock management, use of spaces, activity programmes, giving information and advice, learning programmes, and making judgements about use of resources to target groups, whether from a particular spatial area, age range or interest.
- Providing strategic leadership and advocacy, recognising responsibilities to provide an adequately resourced and proactive library service which influences social and public policy in the local authority area. Developing strategic partnerships regionally and nationally to

progress corporate objectives and the legitimate aspirations of people
and communities.

(Conway, 2008, 6–7)

Conway's report also considered the views of library authorities on the
importance of professional staff:

- Authorities appear to see a reducing role for the professionally chartered
  librarian in the 21st century, as a consequence of a better educated
  population, with increased access to digital information. The role of
  specialists in particular subject areas is questioned.
- Rather the priority is a well trained staff, carrying out agreed procedures,
  proficient in customer care and providing a demand led service.
- In some cases, professional staff were seen by management as being
  opposed to change, inflexible, defensive, often working at inappropriate
  levels and a relatively expensive resource in the context of the service
  budget.

(Conway, 2008, 15)

With such a fresh report the debate is sure to be ongoing; however, it
poses a concern for the future viability of a professional library service
if the professional staff are seen in such limited terms by some senior
officers. What also seems to come out in the responses from authorities
discussed in the report is that deprofessionalization is more about
finances than anything conceptual, which is a major concern; for if short
term financial issues are allowed to dictate the levels of professional staff
and subsequent service quality then there may indeed be a clear
danger to the notion of the professional librarian in many public
library authorities.

Nature of working

Regardless of whether a staff member is professional or paraprofessional,
there are certain qualities, skills and concerns that all public library staff
must be aware of. Some of the topics related to the working situation that
any potential staff considering work in a modern public library service

should consider are discussed below.

- *Project management*: although the day to day running of a library is always of primary concern, many public libraries now deliver some services as projects. This may be because they have bid for and been successful in acquiring money to run a new initiative, or because the initiative they are undertaking is time limited, such as a school holiday campaign for children. Therefore project management skills are essential in professional and paraprofessional supervisory staff, to allow them to undertake their roles.
- *Team work*: every public library worker is part of a team; this may be a team working within a specific library, or a team charged with supporting a specific service function, such as Children's Services. Team work can be rewarding, as individual staff members work with others with different skill sets; however, it can also be stressful if there is group dysfunction, and thus staff members need to understand team dynamics.
- *Opening hours and hours of work*: a consistent criticism from library users is that opening hours are not always suited to their lifestyles. Since the service requires flexibility, staff who wish merely to work a standard nine to five job will find career possibilities in public libraries to be limited mainly to administration tasks. Public libraries often require staff to work at weekends.
- *Part time vs full time*: it is increasingly common to find public libraries employing part-time and casual staff to cover shifts and potential absences. Although undoubtedly useful as a logistical asset, the down side of part-time or casual staffing is that it generally takes longer for new staff to become acquainted with the procedures and stock in the library than for someone who is there full time. Training and induction should address this.
- *Training*: appropriate training is an ongoing concern, and in public libraries that employ many staff it can be a logistical headache. If staff are being trained then it normally means their duties are not being performed, and thus replacements have to be found. This is more of a concern if the staff member has a front-line job or is part of a low staffing complement.

■ *Sickness/absence monitoring*: an unpleasant but necessary human
   resources function for many library managers. If a staff member
   works in the front line it can be a large logistical headache if they have
   a high rate of sickness and absence. Library managers need to be aware
   of the procedure in use in the local authority for supporting staff who
   are ill and ensuring they get any help they may need for problems they
   have.

Hierarchy of needs

In 1954 Maslow proposed a hierarchy of needs that each human being
operates by in the form of a pyramid. He arranged human needs into the
following categories:

■ self-actualization needs
■ esteem needs
■ belonging and love needs
■ safety needs
■ physiological needs.   (Handy, 1993, 33)

At the base of the pyramid are found the basic physiological needs, and
each level increases until at the very top of the pyramid is the self-
actualization needs category. Maslow proposed that each previous need
must be satisfied before the individual can move up to the next level. In
the context of work, as Roberts and Rowley (2004, 73) have suggested,
this means that basic needs such as ample financial reward, safety and
belonging need to be addressed before a person can begin to learn, and
develop their skills. They further highlight this by suggesting that 'a
member of staff would not be motivated by the opportunity for skills
development and learning if their job security is under threat' (Roberts
and Rowley, 2004, 74).

   In terms of physiological needs, the public library authority has a
statutory duty to ensure that the building the staff and public occupy is
safe from hazards and is heated to the appropriate temperature for the
service to be delivered.

Staff safety

Staff in libraries need to be aware of their personal safety and library security. As a public-facing organization staff are occasionally faced with members of the public who are unhappy with the service they have received or with some other aspect of the staff or organization. This rarely but occasionally results in violence.

There has been some analysis of safety issues within libraries carried out in recent years in the USA and the UK (Cravey, 2001; Farrugia, 2002; McGrath and Goulding, 1996; Pease, 1995). In their 1996 survey of UK public libraries McGrath and Goulding found that 69% of staff in the libraries they surveyed had experienced a library user who had been verbally abusive, only 8% had experienced physical abuse, but 21% had experienced sexual harassment (McGrath and Goulding, 1996, 5). Farrugia (2002) suggests that libraries must have policies in place for dealing with what has been dubbed the profession's 'skeleton in the closet' (Easton, 1977, quoted in McGrath and Goulding, 1996).

Cravey offers a thorough analysis of library security, from ensuring that the collections are secure from damage, theft and natural disasters, through to ensuring staff and user safety within and outside the library premises. Certainly for the public library manager security is a major concern that should be taken very seriously, and staff and user safety must be of paramount importance from a duty of care perspective.

Career structure

In their 2001 study of the public library workforce Usherwood et al. found that career stagnation was a crucial demotivator for many members of public library staff (Usherwood et al., 2001). The convention was that there was little turnover of staff within the public library sector with the result that not only was it difficult for prospective new entrants to get into the sector, but once they were there progression through the ranks was difficult. As one respondent to the focus groups set up as part of the project suggested, 'once you are in public libraries you are there for life' (Usherwood et al., 2001, 121). The reduction in the number of professional posts we have seen over the past ten years exacerbates this situation.

One of the ironies of career progression within public libraries is that the duties and work that motivate people to go into the profession in the first place are different from the tasks required of those who move through the levels of the structure. As more professional posts are usually in policy areas, those holding them no longer spend much time working with the public, a part of the job that was one of the key motivators for many professional staff to enter the profession in the first place.

Clearly such posts continue to have rewards, as organizing policy related to children's work, adult services or reader development across an entire group of libraries, which can then be carried out by specialist members of your team or front line staff, has major rewards. But opportunities for being at the front line of service delivery are more limited than they were in the past for those in such posts.

Conclusion

The professional concerns of the public librarian have remained relatively consistent: ensuring that the library user has access to the best possible reading and information sources for their need, that the material is efficiently and professionally selected and managed, and that the service is delivered courteously and with respect. The professional librarian must also consider their responsibility to society in delivering the information, and ensure that the service they provide is enhancing society and not damaging it.

However, modern ways of managing public services have challenged the notion of the professional and the desirability of having professionally qualified librarians to the same levels as in the past. These notions are sadly primarily about finance rather than concept, notwithstanding justifications such as requiring staff with people skills. Librarianship has always been a profession that is about helping people, and the library user is far more efficiently served by a knowledgeable, qualified professional than someone who may be excellent in customer service but knows little about the library stock and how best to use it for the benefit of the user.

Thus debates around deprofessionalization are not merely about how to deliver library services most efficiently, they are crucial in ensuring there are high quality and knowledgeable staff who are best equipped to aid library users within the information society.

References

CILIP (2004) *Body of Professional Knowledge*, www.cilip.org.uk/NR/rdonlyres/3CA8898C-902F-4B1F-AE07-58B0BAE6AEB2/0/BPK.pdf.

Conway, P. (2008) *Professional Standards of Service*, CILIP, www.cilip.org.uk/policyadvocacy/statements/conwayreport/.

Cravey, P. J. (2001) *Protecting Library Staff, Users, Collections and Facilities: a how to do it manual for librarians*, Neal-Schuman.

Creaser, C., Maynard, S. and White, S. (2006) *LISU Annual Library Statistics*, Library and Information Statistics Unit.

Dixon, D., Duffy, A., Fuller, R. and McGrath, F. (2005) *Basic Reference Resources for the Public Library*, 5th edn, Information Services Group.

Farrugia, S. (2002) A Dangerous Occupation? Violence in public libraries, *New Library World*, **103** (9), 309-19.

Handy, C. (1993) *Understanding Organizations*, 4th edn, Penguin.

ISG (1999) *Guidelines for Reference and Information Services in Public Libraries*, Library Association Publishing.

McGrath, H. and Goulding, A. (1996) Part of the Job: violence in libraries, *New Library World*, **97** (3), 4-13.

Pease, B. (1995) Workplace Violence in Libraries, *Library Management*, **16** (7), 30-9.

Roberts, S. and Rowley, J. (2004) *Managing Information Services*, Facet Publishing.

Usherwood, B., Proctor, R., Bower, G., Coe, C., Cooper, J. and Stevens, T. (2001) *Recruit, Retain and Lead: the public library workforce study*, Centre for the Public Library and Information in Society, Department of Information Studies, University of Sheffield and Resource.

Chapter 11

Marketing, branding and buildings

Introduction

Several key challenges present themselves to the public librarian when marketing their services in the modern era. As the services on offer could be seen to compete with other social, educational, information, cultural and leisure opportunities members of the public have available to them, public libraries must increasingly use marketing techniques to spread the message of what they have on offer. This has led to debates related to what libraries are, what services they should provide, and even whether the word library itself is a positive or negative thing.

This chapter will discuss the key issues related to the marketing of public library services in the 21st century, and how modern approaches to branding are being used to reinvent the public library concept. It will also discuss the issue of library buildings, and how an ageing infrastructure is being perceived as a barrier to service progression by many library services.

Marketing public libraries

Public library professionals need to take marketing very seriously in the modern age. The challenge is twofold: marketing to the library user community and marketing upwards to senior officers and elected members.

As Usherwood has stated, it 'is necessary for public librarians to exercise effective public relations if they are to obtain recognition and support at both national and local level' (Usherwood, 1989, 29). Advocacy, then, is as important within the local authority structure as it is to the user community.

Nevertheless there are few services that have the entire population as their potential membership base, yet this is the reality for public library services. In theory a public library can have a potential membership level of 100% of the people who live in the community served. Since public libraries also serve people who work or study in a specific area, and many also offer services to tourists, we see a potential market that puts other publicly funded services in the shade. Of course the reality is that public libraries would be unable to cope with such a high demand, but this in itself offers challenges in terms of which audiences the marketing of library services should be addressed at.

Public library user as customer?

Libraries exist around providing services to users; in this way they can be compared to the service industries such as retail, catering and other leisure industries. Indeed some commentators have argued that when discussing libraries and users we should adopt the language of the private sector and refer to library users as customers (Koontz, 2002). Another commentator on library marketing issues has argued that 'Librarians and information professionals are in the people business' (de Saez, 2002, 1).

This approach has serious dissenters within the profession, however, with prominent commentators such as Buschman and Usherwood arguing that use of terms like customer devalue a relationship that is built on benefit to the community (Buschman, 2003; Usherwood, 2007). It is an important distinction to note that public libraries are not commercial entities in any sense of the word. They are not selling products that must be sold for the organization to remain viable. As a social educational vehicle for their communities they provide resources based on user need, and do not limit service provision to those who can afford to pay. This is a crucial distinction to make in terms of service identity, and although there are certainly lessons to be learned from how the private sector markets its products to customers, it would be a fundamental error to assume that marketing to customers and marketing to library users is the same thing.

In the case of marketing a commercial product the remit is not always to sell to people who need it but merely to sell; for commercial reality means that convincing them they need the product is a crucial aspect of marketing, and sophisticated advertising is employed to do just that. Marketing to library users involves similar techniques, but the emphasis is on raising awareness of services that users may actually need. There is little point in a public service if capacity is wasted in providing services to people who do not require them. This is the key difference between selling someone a product and marketing them a public service.

The four Ps of marketing

One of the most well known aspects of marketing theory relates to what is known as the four Ps, otherwise known as the marketing mix. The four Ps are:

- product
- price
- place
- promotion.

These obviously commercial terms relate to public libraries in various ways:

- *Product*: in the context of libraries, the product is whatever the user needs. In a public library it can be the latest Harry Potter book; a DVD film or a music CD; or it can even be an entire range of stock. There are many *products* that are produced when a library service is provided.
- *Price*: for many libraries this is the most problematic of the four Ps. As de Saez suggests, 'Price is the element of the marketing mix which for many in the library profession will be the most difficult to consider' and price does not necessarily equate to a cash value (de Saez, 2002, 67). The price could be defined as the cost to the taxpayer of the service. Therefore although most public library services are free at the point of use, there is still a price to be paid for that service by the library user.

- *Place*: this is another concept that is changing as technology continues to improve. In the past, place would have been the physical library building, but in the modern world place can be a website or a digital library.
- *Promotion*: this is perhaps the aspect of marketing that librarians have had to learn to be more proactive about. In many libraries marketing budgets can be small, and thus competing with the sophisticated marketing of companies that spend lots of money on promotion can be a challenge.

Attracting users

Public libraries operate in a quandary: they aim to provide services to everyone who lives, works or studies in the area they are responsible for, but in reality usage is limited. The danger then is that the service continually provides more and more services aimed at the users it actually has rather than diversifies to attract the users it does not.

Of course there are myriad reasons why potential users may not see the public library as offering them anything they require, either through lack of knowledge of what is provided by the service, or because they do not need what is on offer. If we consider the avid reader who is able to afford to purchase the books they require, what exactly can the library use to draw that person in?

Challenges of marketing public libraries

While undoubtedly institutions that have a positive role in their communities, public libraries also suffer from an image problem that is consistently communicated through media representations of librarians and public libraries as old-fashioned, staid and serious. The image of the bespectacled spinster or bachelor dispensing novels with a stern request for silence is one that is hard to shift, even if the profession itself is aware of its lack of reality.

Public librarians also need to be aware that many potential adult borrowers may have had user experiences as children that were not positive. There was a period in the past in many public libraries where on entering a library building a child would be greeted with the question as to whether or not they had washed their hands before coming in. As that child grows into an adult such experiences may not positively induce them towards seeing the library as a place where they want to spend time.

Leisure time has more options

Modern life presents many more opportunities for people to use their leisure time than it did in the past. If we recall one of the key reasons why the 1850 Act was passed, it was related to ensuring that the working classes had something more productive to do with their time than drink alcohol. Notwithstanding that particular activity remaining popular, the average citizen has many more ways of spending time in enjoyment of their leisure time now than in 1850, and most have more of it. With other cultural attractions such as theatre and cinema, sporting activities such as gyms and other fitness hobbies remaining popular, and as disposable incomes have increased, more potential library users are now able to purchase for their reading needs rather than needing to borrow from the library.

In a small scale study on the reasons for the decline in borrowing of books in Scottish public libraries, respondents who did not borrow books were asked for some of the reasons why they did not use the library. 52% said they accessed the books they required elsewhere, 32% stated that they were too busy to visit the library, 29% were dissatisfied with the book selection, and 27% were unhappy with opening hours. Other reasons that were posited by smaller proportions of the respondents included the preference to do other things (23%), and the location of the library (20%) (Breslin and McMenemy, 2006, 422).

A recent study into the perceptions of public libraries of people in the age group 14–35 suggested that for non-users 'negative perceptions of libraries are fairly deeply entrenched' (MLA, DCMS and LASER, 2006, 5). The report suggested that only public libraries whose infrastructure and service had been modernized had potential interest for non-users in the age group. A positive finding was that for some non-users who had not visited a modernized library the realization of what the modern service had to offer changed 'their perceptions of public libraries'.

Love Libraries campaign

A recent groundbreaking campaign has sought to market the public library on a national scale. Love Libraries (www.lovelibraries.co.uk) 'is a campaign to get everyone excited about what public libraries have to offer. With millions of free books, newspapers, CDs, DVDs, audio tapes, internet terminals, author events, reading groups and much much more, libraries have something to offer for everyone.'

The partnership consisted of The Reading Agency, nine publishers, the MLA, DCMS and Society of Chief Librarians, and aimed to raise awareness of library services and widen their appeal. A major strategy was to enlist celebrities and authors as celebrity supporters to provide comments on why they valued libraries and why they were so important to society. Members of the public were also sought to be library champions and provide their viewpoints on the importance of the service to them. Launched in spring 2006, another of its first initiatives was to transform three libraries in separate authorities in a 12-week period.

Other initiatives undertaken by the campaign include an annual Top Ten New Librarians Award, to highlight some of the up and coming staff in libraries and their achievements. There is also an annual Love Libraries Award which is voted on online via the campaign website, with members of the public asked to select the winner. The 2007 Award went to Lancaster Library, which has sought to widen its appeal to younger people by offering music performances within the library by up and coming bands.

Mission statements

A positive way that the library can promote what it is about is by using a mission statement. A mission statement communicates in a simple way what the goal of the organization is and what its aims are for the service it provides.

A mission statement should use clear and uncluttered language and communicate without professional or political jargon. Mission statements are normally displayed prominently within library buildings and are increasingly being placed on the library web pages.

It is useful to look in more detail at how some libraries in the UK are promoting their mission to users. The statement for the Kent County

Council Libraries and Archives states that their goal is 'to enhance the quality of life for all Kent's residents and communities, by stimulating lifelong imagination, exploration and discovery' (Kent County Council, 2003). The mission of the Cornwall County Council library service is to:

- be the most reliable source of information in Cornwall
- promote reading, learning and the latest information technology to everybody in Cornwall
- celebrate Cornwall's unique culture and heritage.

(Cornwall County Council, n.d.)

Ceredigion County Council has a fuller statement than either of the two previously mentioned:

> The public library is a major community facility whose purpose is to enable and encourage individuals or groups of individuals to gain unbiased access to books, information, knowledge and works of creative imagination which will:

- Encourage their active participation in cultural, democratic and economic activities
- Enable them to participate in educational development through formal or informal programmes
- Assist them to make positive use of leisure time
- Promote reading and literacy as basic skills necessary for active involvement in these activities
- Encourage the use of information and an awareness of its value.

(Ceredigion County Council, 2008)

Thus we can see different approaches to how a mission is communicated, but in all three cases we see similar aims presented for the service. Consistent throughout is community enhancement and development through the use of the service, encouragement and promotion of reading and discovery, and commitment to freedom of access and expression.

Branding and rebranding

Branding of services is something we probably take for granted. We are bombarded daily with advertisements for a myriad of branded products and services. Development of a brand can be a costly enterprise for companies who seek to maximize their attraction to the public by developing brand recognition. It could be argued that public libraries have suffered over the years for not having what could be described as an identifiable brand, or suffered for having a brand that communicated negative and old-fashioned messages to potential users. Equally for the users who enjoy using public libraries the brand for them may well be positive.

Roberts and Rowley suggest that a 'brand can be viewed as the seller's promise to consistently deliver a specific set of benefits, values, or attributes to the consumer' (Roberts and Rowley, 2004, 141). Creation of a brand is designed not merely as a tool for selling a service, but also as a stamp of quality. With the brand is communicated a set of standards that the user will become familiar with, and thus any deviation from that norm will not merely reflect badly on the single service that has failed, but also on the entire brand. For instance, purchasing a television set of a particular brand that constantly needs to be repaired is unlikely to see you purchasing that brand again. Instead of associating the brand with a quality item the association becomes a poor one. This is why branding, while a potentially useful marketing tool, can also be a potentially dangerous one unless a quality service can be guaranteed.

As will be discussed below, rebranding has taken place in several public library services (Hood and Henderson, 2005). The reasons for this have mainly related to perceptions of libraries among the user community and the negative image many of the potential users have held of public libraries which led to lack of use.

Discovery centres

An example of rebranding of public library services are 'discovery centres'. An initiative of Hampshire County Council, discovery centres are 'an exciting new development providing an opportunity for more people to use our wide range of services' (Hampshire County Council, 2008). The goal of the authority is to build on the three centres already in place in the county to enhance provision to the local community. The marketing of the centres suggests to users that they are more than just a library, emphasizing the wider use of the facilities that go beyond traditional library services. As well as a library, the Winchester Discovery Centre includes a performance hall and exhibition spaces, while the Gosport Discovery Centre also houses a museum.

Idea stores

In Tower Hamlets chronic under-use of the public library service led library managers to adopt a radical approach to service provision, and as part of a major rebranding initiative the libraries were renamed idea stores. The issue was larger than simply renaming, however, and a £20 million investment was announced to create a network of high quality modern facilities for the area. At the root of the idea was a retail concept, and the initiative promised users that:

- We are committed to a major investment programme to modernize your libraries and adult education services.
- The Idea Stores will be built where people will use them – and can get to them easily.
- We will only merge existing libraries and adult education centres once the new Idea Stores are up and running.
- We will develop a truly customer-focused service.
- In contrast to many other areas of Britain, we are committed to a major investment programme to modernize your libraries – having already doubled our spend on books in recent years and invested hundreds of thousands of pounds in new IT facilities.
- We aim to achieve seven-day-a-week opening – already in operation at the existing Idea Stores.

(Tower Hamlets Council, 2007)

Such initiatives are not without their critics: one commentator has suggested that when he visited an idea store:

The atmosphere was a cross between supermarket and budget-airline lounge and the attendance was desultory. Any sense of the numinous, any urge for self-improvement had been lost in transition. Alarmingly, large book stocks had been dumped en route. . . . The anti-elitists and design lobbyists behind these Ideas Stores might as well have thrown the books on a bonfire.

(Lebrecht, 2006, 36)

It is vital that rebranding does not alienate old library users to gain the new, although as with any change there are likely always to be those who oppose it. The challenge of creating a modern library service that appeals to all user groups without losing users who advocate a traditional feel to the service and user environment is constant.

Challenges in infrastructure and location

The physical condition of a library can have an immense impact on users. In the 2004–5 Parliamentary Session, the House of Commons Committee on Culture, Media and Sport produced a report on public libraries that highlighted library buildings as one of the major challenges facing the sector. It stated that 'evidence was clear that a significant barrier to library use was shabby buildings' (Culture, Media and Sport Committee, 2005, 31). In the evidence considered by the Committee the total cost to correct the buildings across the UK was estimated as between £240 million and £650 million.

Library buildings – hindrance or asset?

Library buildings are perhaps the most visible way of promoting a quality service to the library user, and are therefore of immense importance. Unfortunately, because of their long history, many public library buildings across the country are old, some dating from the early Carnegie era and earlier. These buildings while being magnificent public institutions pose major problems when modernizing and upgrading the infrastructure.

Reinforce old views about elitism?

Another argument against older library buildings is that they communicate a negative image to potential users. There is some truth in this concept, since the design of many incorporated classical architecture and attempted to communicate through classical imagery the values of a previous period and what the library building represented to the people of the time, namely knowledge and education . Unfortunately a criticism of these buildings in the modern era is that they can be off-putting and communicate what is perceived to be an elitist sentiment to users. This is a concern that must be taken seriously. Communicating the mission of the library within a modern, pleasing and aesthetic environment is the goal.

Carnegie buildings

In Chapter 2 we discussed the legacy of Andrew Carnegie and the impact his philanthropy had on public library development in the UK and USA, but for many public library services the existence of Carnegie libraries brings challenges. While undoubtedly being beautiful buildings of historic importance, their status as landmarks can make it difficult to redevelop them.

For instance, there are a large number of older library buildings including many Carnegie builds that are listed buildings, which means there are legally binding restrictions on alterations to their facade and infrastructure. This was a problem that led to increased costs for several public library authorities when undertaking work on the infrastructure for the People's Network. It also means that major modernization of the interior is at least problematic, and in extreme circumstances impossible.

Location, location, location

Many public library buildings are not in prominent or attractive locations. Many older buildings were at the heart of their community when they were built, but often communities evolve, and as new houses and other amenities are built the library building position today is often on the edge of where the majority of a community now resides or shops. This is especially true of public library buildings constructed in what were previously shopping thoroughfares, as the move away from high street shopping to US-style strip malls or large supermarkets has led to many former bustling high streets being underused. This has a knock-on effect for the traffic passing the library, and visiting the library can become something that takes special effort rather than being something a user did while out shopping.

Another challenge of location is the desire the Government has expressed to see local authority service points merging. This was one of the main recommendations of the DCMS 1999 policy paper, *Libraries for All*, which suggested that the social inclusion agenda would be better serviced by co-hosting libraries within buildings containing other services. There are numerous examples of this; one of the most recent award-winning initiatives is a complex in the east-end community of Easterhouse in Glasgow called The Bridge.

This is a wide-ranging partnership between the local further education college, the local authority's culture and sport department, and arts organizations, which have formed an integrated service for the community. People in the local community can use the library, visit the theatre, swim, and undertake fitness classes and formal learning. The facility has won several design awards and, perhaps more important, usage has been brisk within the community. The new library has become one of the top six libraries in the city; the previous library had been in 24th position. Visitor figures increased by 242%, book issues by 27%, and ICT usage by 51%, suggesting that the new facility was attractive to the local community.

The Library at the Bridge is an excellent example of how joint-use facilities can enhance the experience of accessing public services for an entire community. In the case of this project it was not merely a case of merging service points; thought was put into how each aspect of the merged facility could complement the others, and it is common for library initiatives to lead to users entering college courses, or taking part in theatre workshops.

Better Public Libraries

In 2003 a joint publication between Resource and the Centre for Architecture and the Built Environment (CABE) looked at the issue of library buildings. In their publication *Better Public Libraries* they featured a table highlighting what they perceived to be the differences between traditional library architecture and modern library architecture (Table 11.1).

Table 11.1 Better Public Libraries – comparison between old and new library architecture

Traditional library architecture	Modern library architecture
Neo Classical pattern book	Modern free style
Imposing steps and entrance halls	Street level, retail entrances
Needs of disabled people unmet	Good disability access
Domes and rotunda	Atriums and top-floor cafés
Galleries and mezzanines	Escalators and lifts
Clerestory light	Atrium light
Restricted access to books	Open access to books and other materials
Bookshelves requiring ladders	Bookshelves at human scale
Temple of knowledge	The 'living room in the city'
Institutional furniture	Domestic or club furniture
Stand alone building	Shared space with other services
Hierarchical design and circulation	Open-plan design and circulation
Canonical stock-holding	Contemporary cultural market-place
Individual study carrels	Seminar rooms and computer suites
Defensive space	Networked space
Librarians as knowledge custodians	Librarians as knowledge navigators
The rule of silence	The culture of mutual respect
Child free	Child friendly

Although some of the accusations against traditional library architecture in the document seem sweeping, for example allowing only restricted access to books, the rule of silence and that they should be child free, it is evident that the discourse around traditional library buildings is a negative one for many users and in policy circles. They are perceived as barriers to an inclusive and modern service and therefore should be considered as part of any marketing strategy aimed at attracting disenfranchised users.

New library builds

As has been discussed in Chapter 8, there have been significant opportunities for local authorities over the past ten years or so to tap into private sector funding for building new public facilities through the Government's Private Finance Initiative (PFI) programme. This has run in conjunction with the desire by many authorities to fund construction of joint-use facilities of the kind discussed above, which has led to a healthy number of new library builds in the period.

The Designing Libraries (www.designinglibraries.org.uk/) project maintains an extensive database of new library builds and library redesign projects in the UK, offering data on the project, square footage and design details, and in many cases images of the finished product. Featuring over 150 new library build listings on the database across sectors it illustrates that the past ten years have been an active period in library building construction.

Conclusion

Undoubtedly public libraries now have more competition from other leisure facilities and users and potential users have more leisure time than they had in the past. This reinforces the need to ensure that marketing is undertaken to raise awareness of the public library and what it has to offer the members of its community.

Yet marketing public libraries is a challenging endeavour. Public libraries are open to all, yet providing services for and marketing to all potential users is not a realistic notion. Therefore the librarian must decide who best to target among its user community, and marketing initiatives must be properly managed and evaluated for effectiveness.

Recent national campaigns such as Love Libraries and other work undertaken by The Reading Agency, such as the partnership with the Richard & Judy Book Club, also help raise the profile of library services to a wider audience. If non-users have a negative perception of the library service, then positive marketing and campaigning can help improve this image.

The increased interest in the aesthetics of libraries and the design of their exteriors and interiors shows that the service can market itself to users in a positive way. The creation of welcoming and warm spaces and enhancement of services by offering joint-use service points means that library users can better use their limited free time by visiting the library and undertaking other social or educational activities. Such joint-use services offer a truly socially inclusive environment.

References

Breslin, F. and McMenemy, D. (2006) The Decline in Book Borrowing from Britain's Public Libraries: a small scale Scottish study, *Library Review*, **55** (7), 414-28.

Buschman, J. E. (2003) *Dismantling the Public Sphere: situating and sustaining librarianship in the age of the new public philosophy*, Libraries Unlimited.

Ceredigion County Council (2008) *Library Mission Statement*, www.ceredigion.gov.uk/index.cfm?articleid=440.

Cornwall County Council (n.d.) *Library Mission Statement*, www.cornwall.gov.uk/index.cfm?articleid=5666.

Culture, Media and Sport Committee (2005) *Public Libraries: third report of Session 2004-2005*, Culture, Media and Sport Committee, House of Commons.

DCMS (1999) *Libraries for All: social inclusion in public libraries*, Department for Culture, Media and Sport.

de Saez, E. E. (2002) *Marketing Concepts for Libraries and Information Services*, 2nd edn, Facet Publishing.

Future Libraries Partnership (2006) *Love Libraries: the libraries*, www.lovelibraries.co.uk/libraries.php.

Hampshire County Council (2008) *Discovery Centres Are More Than Just Libraries*, www3.hants.gov.uk/discoverycentres.

Hood, D. and Henderson, K. (2005) Branding in the UK Public Library Service, *New Library World*, **106** (1/2), 16-28.

Kent County Council (2003) *Libraries and Archives Mission Statement*, www.kent.gov.uk/NR/rdonlyres/1202B3CB-8D25-4F43-8FC2-C4503BDA8D01/3284/MissionStatementCoreobjectives.pdf.

Koontz, C. (2002) Stores and Libraries: both serve customers, *Marketing Library Services*, **16** (1), www.ugr.es/~alozano/Translations/Koontz.htm.

Lebrecht, N. (2006) Vandals At The Museum's Door, *Evening Standard*, 29 March, 36.

MLA, DCMS and LASER (2006) *A Research Study of 14-35 year olds for the Future Development of Public Libraries*,

www.bl.uk/aboutus/acrossuk/workpub/laser/publications/
projreports/publiclibraries.pdf.

Resource and CABE (2003) *Better Public Libraries*, Resource and the
Centre for Architecture and the Built Environment,
www.mla.gov.uk/resources/assets//I/id874rep_pdf_6757.pdf.

Roberts, S. and Rowley, J. (2004) *Managing Information Services*, Facet
Publishing.

Tower Hamlets Council (2007) *Idea Stores*,
www.ideastore.co.uk.

Usherwood, B. (1989) *The Public Library as Public Knowledge*, Library
Association Publishing.

Usherwood, B. (2007) *Equity and Excellence in the Public Library: why
ignorance is not our heritage*, Ashgate.

Chapter 12

Conclusion: the public library of tomorrow

Introduction

This text has sought to discuss the nature of the services on offer in the modern public library, where those services originated from, and how librarians have dealt with the service challenges facing them in the modern era. This final chapter will reflect on all of this and pose some questions for the future; as a result it may appear more polemical in tone than the chapters that have preceded it as it seeks to ask some fundamental questions.

Predicting what will happen to public libraries over the years to come is a difficult endeavour. Certainly voices predicting their demise seem to be built on flimsy foundations, but equally it would be a brave commentator who argued that the future will be completely trouble-free and rosy. How society is synthesizing information is changing in a revolutionary way and public libraries may or may not fit into that. There is, however, an in-built ignorance in doomsayers who predict the demise of public libraries. The drop in book issues is a definite cause for concern, but in truth they should never have been used as the primary benchmark for the success of public libraries, and in a world where the modern person has a multitude of calls on their leisure time it seems complacent in the extreme to do so.

Public libraries: an outdated concept?

The first question that society and the profession will have to consider is whether the public library is a concept that has served its purpose. The original reasons why they were introduced could be argued to be of lesser importance today, since literacy and numeracy rates are now much higher than they were in the Victorian era. Book prices have come down considerably, especially since the collapse of the Net Book Agreement in the 1990s. Thus many more people are now able to afford books than they could even 20 years ago.

Equally, however, the concerns with ensuring that everyone is able to access the best materials have not in any way dissipated. Although many can afford to buy what they need, many still cannot, and without a public library service they would be excluded from accessing the materials that enhance their life through the enjoyment of the recreational, learning and cultural experiences that libraries provide. In all of the discourse around the diminishing use of public library services it is crucial not to lose sight of the fact that many people within our communities continue to need the services they offer.

Revisiting service themes

The categories used in the discussion of service themes within the book were equity of access, cultural and leisure roles, information and informed citizenship, and lifelong learning. Revisiting these themes once more seems apt in this concluding chapter.

Equity of access

Even in the most democratic of nations the public library is one of the few impartial public spaces that remain. Alongside museums they remain public institutions that offer a place of quiet consideration of knowledge and humanity, free from the pressure of day to day life, where a user can browse the shelves.

Yet equity of access is something that is regularly under attack from both economic and moral perspectives. The debate was reiterated in 1986 by *Ex Libris* questions on whether the public purse should fund access, and this political question will continue to be asked. Yet the public library remains a vital contributor to democratic life through its mission of equity, freedom of expression, and opposition to censorship of all kinds.

Cultural and leisure roles

The public library's role in the promotion of reading and literacy is of vital importance to the cultural fabric of the nation. Through the myriad initiatives aimed at children and young people public librarians can help foster a love of reading and the book that will stand them in good stead for the remainder of their life. When children's minds are opened to the joy of reading, their access to the world of books will ensure that they will be able to enlarge their aspirations and develop a broader world view beyond that of their own surroundings.

Equally, through the techniques of reader development adults can have their reading choices expanded, and their tastes widened through good advice and high quality book selection by library staff. In addition, library organized reading groups can enhance their enjoyment of what they read as they share their views with friends and other members of their community, offering an intellectual and social element to the reading experience and enhancing community engagement.

Information and informed citizenship

A school of thought evident in some responses to the Conway Report suggested that the role of the public library in information provision is diminished as a result of the internet and world wide web. It is truly astonishing to see such views emanating from people responsible for administering public library services, and bodes the question of how well they themselves actually know the internet and accuracy of the information therein. The need for high quality and accurate information sources is as stark in the digital age as it was in the analogue, and the need for public libraries to ensure the public have access to definitive and well sourced reference works is crucial. Crucially, the role of the public library in embracing information literacy for its users is of paramount importance. Information is advocated by schools, colleges and universities, and public libraries as a sector must increase the emphasis on information literacy training for their users.

An information literate community relies on the public library to act as a gateway to responsible and accurate information, and that need is as vital as it always has been. Informed citizens recognize the limitations of the internet and do not embrace it as a panacea.

Lifelong learning

Notions of the public library as a streetcorner university may be overstating things a little, but there is no doubt that, for generations of people since libraries were first made freely available to the public, they have allowed an informal educational experience to take place. Recent moves to build on this educational role of public libraries have included attempts to formalize it through the teaching of qualifications such as the ECDL, which offer library users a tangible end product for their efforts.

Notwithstanding this, public libraries will continue to offer an informal space for people to learn new skills and knowledge through texts and now increasingly through ICTs. This informal learning that takes place is an invaluable service to the community and must continue to be supported formally, through the continued acquisition of non-fiction and learning materials, and informally through a constant reinforcement of this role as a key public library mission.

Predictions of demise

The first decade of the 21st century has seen a plethora of studies into the public library, from government blueprints for success, to calls asking 'Who's in charge?'. All represent a necessary quest for an understanding of the public library mission in the 21st century.

It could be argued that a key reason for the negative discourse prevalent around libraries is the use of scientific management techniques to extrapolate usage statistics into the future. The result is headline-grabbing news such as, 'UK Libraries out of use by 2020' (BBC News, 2004). Although such headlines certainly create a debate, there is a risk that they do more damage than good, since they suggest a culture of under-performance, failure and underachievement, which is grossly unhealthy and also unfair to the public library staff who see beyond issue statistics and make positive contributions to the lives of members of their community every day.

More positively, marketing campaigns such as Love Libraries promote the good things happening in libraries by advancing a message that the public can buy into. Rather than suggesting people are about to lose their library, campaigns like Love Libraries tell them what is going on in a positive way and remind them just what public libraries have to offer them. The sector needs more campaigns like Love Libraries, and less navel gazing about apocalyptic scenarios based on mathematical gymnastics rather than any sense of reality.

Book borrowing levels are important but they do not define an entire service in the way that reports predicting the demise of the public library suggest they do. Rather than merely focusing on those who do not borrow, the profession needs to take more cognizance of the impact of the service on those who do. Here the movement towards more qualitative methods of self-evaluation suggests that a more holistic understanding of the true impact of libraries on the community is tantalizingly close.

Public libraries: lessons from retail?

In previous chapters we have discussed the calls for public libraries to learn lessons from the retail sector and the subsequent initiatives that have sought to use the retail model in service delivery and design.

A commercial imperative?

In the era of new public management (NPM) the pressure to raise revenues in even the most benign of public services has increased in importance. Not only has the call to be commercial by raising revenue increased, the suggestion that public libraries need to ape the commercial sector more closely in terms of how they look, act and measure their value has also increased.

Public libraries do not exist to make money, and any emphases in this direction run the danger of changing how public libraries are perceived by the public. In Chapter 8 we discussed the trend towards income generation, from its simplest forms in selling reading glasses and stationery, through to selling access to advertisers to provide direct mail to library users. Such initiatives must be handled carefully if the public is not to begin to perceive the library as a place that is no longer free of commercial influence. Political realities may necessitate aping the private sector model, although the logical end result of this policy taken too far is that the public begins to perceive the public library in the same way they do the private sector. Although this may bring slick, high quality advertising and service points, what we may lose on the way is something fundamentally more important.

In his speech at the 2007 American Library Association Conference, Garrison Keillor described the public library as 'one of the noblest expressions of democracy, still' (Keillor, 2007). It will only remain so by maintaining its core values as a place of knowledge and learning; a place where anyone can feel welcome, be valued as a citizen not a customer, and be provided with a service with no hidden agenda.

Public library users *must* be seen by the profession as citizens and not consumers, for if that relationship is altered then the nature of the service provided changes with it. The attitude of a profession towards the people it serves is fundamental to the entire service encounter. If a user is seen as someone the professionals wish to help to get the best out of the service, rather than someone they wish to sell something to, then the values and integrity of the public library will be maintained.

More debate and discussion within the profession needs to take place about how much the private sector can actually influence the public library in a positive way. Until now the tacit assumption based on political priorities has been that this is unequivocally a good thing, but this concept cannot go under-researched and unchallenged. We must seek to understand what these changes mean on a deeper level if we are to ensure we take the best from them.

The equity and excellence debate

In 2007 Bob Usherwood published a highly passionate plea for public libraries to refocus their energies on ensuring that they are equitable institutions centred around ensuring the public has access to quality (Usherwood, 2007).

He rightly raises the spectre of our dumbing down as a society as a clear danger to the values of libraries, and his concern over the managerialist mantra of giving people what they want rather than what they may need is one all professionals should ponder. In a country where a recent survey shows that children under ten value as the three most important things in the world being a celebrity, good looks and being rich, there is a concern about the nature of the values society is transmitting to its young people (Johnson and McSmith, 2006).

The profession must seek to ensure that in currying political favour and a wide popular appeal it does not lose sight of quality and the importance of access to that quality that communities need. People cannot become lifelong learners if materials for learning have been denigrated at the altar of pulp fiction or celebrity biographies to ensure borrower figures remain healthy. The key is that public libraries should contain a balanced collection that offers the popular alongside the worthy and the great.

Public libraries and ICTs

The ongoing struggle between those who plant themselves firmly in the book camp and those who plant themselves in the ICT camp is damaging for the future of the service. It is interesting that such mindsets have long ago been excised from academic librarianship, which has seen far more of an impact from ICTs than the public library, to the benefit of all stakeholders.

Books will always be the staple of the public library; far more people use the library to borrow books than for any other purpose. This does not make it any more important to the people who do so than accessing ICTs or reading a newspaper for those who choose to undertake that activity instead. Access to the best should mean access to the best books, information, ICTs, staff, periodicals and multimedia.

Education of public librarians

The biggest threat to the long term viability of the public library is related to how the staff who deliver it are educated and trained, and the skills and knowledge they have. The creeping deprofessionalization that is being seen in some UK authorities is a result of short-term political and financial expediency rather than any conceptual approach to libraries and service delivery.

The discourse of managerialism paints the professions in a negative light; they are continually discussed in the literature as being behind the times, against change and unwilling to take risks to transform services. Not surprisingly, then, the findings from the Conway Report saw some authorities paint professional librarians as set in their ways, obstacles to change and overall more trouble than they are worth. Such attitudes are regrettable and need to be challenged by the collective profession rather than individual librarians within library services.

We can certainly see that the role of the librarian has remained relatively constant in the history of libraries in the UK. An irony is that we have almost come full circle from the early days when public librarianship struggled for professional status as it begins to do again in several library authorities in the 21st century.

A definite loss for the wider profession and society is the decline in scholarly activity of librarians, something that throughout the 20th century saw county and city librarians pen wonderful thought pieces within the professional literature. Perhaps it is the nature of the duties changing inexorably, but it would be positive to see more senior officers within public libraries rediscover the concept of the scholar librarian and contribute to wider professional debate in the same ways their predecessors did. Indeed the question would be whether modern practical concerns would allow a head of service to be able to contribute in the ways Lionel McColvin and others did throughout their professional careers.

The public library and librarian of the future

Then what of the services that will be on offer in the public library of the future: how will they differ? By far the most popular reason for using a public library among the majority of the population is to borrow books, and, as tastes change, the types of books people borrow may well change with them. The consistent thing will be the venue where the public know they can borrow the material they want, and the material they need for the different life challenges they face.

Public libraries need public librarians to develop the services they offer. Despite a managerial discourse that sees professionals in a negative light the role of the professional librarian is crucial if the public is to get the best from their library service.

Political priorities

As services provided by politically governed institutions at a local level, and legally responsible to politically governed institutions at a national level, public libraries cannot avoid politics. What they must be careful of, however, is becoming too close to the political doctrines of one particular party at the expense of their impartiality.

Although the rhetoric of the current UK Government has played well with the wider profession as it allowed public libraries to argue their role as key institutions for delivering political priorities such as social inclusion, this may not continue if a change in administration occurs at a national level. In many ways if this does occur it will be a step into the unknown and any professional discourse that appears too closely allied to a previous administration may well put the sector at a political disadvantage.

Conclusion

Public libraries have served the British public for longer than the 158 years since they were formalized in the first legislation. They have enhanced communities, offered access to the best for anyone in the population who aspires to read high quality works of the imagination and fact, and allowed unbiased access to information to enhance citizenship.

They stand as testaments to the aspirations of a nation to whom fairness and parity has been a political ideal for generations. As society changes the pressure on the public library service to do likewise remains strong, but change must not alter core values. The reason that the UK still can boast over 4500 public libraries is because the public likes the service, and continues to want it. Aspirations to improve service quality should always be drivers for the profession, but short-termism and changes for the sake of change are potentially dangerous. The profession needs to begin again to value public libraries as much as the general public still does, and challenge negativity and politically motivated sniping from the sidelines.

Britons have a right to be proud of their public libraries, and the public library profession has an equal right to be proud of that fact.

References

BBC News (2004) UK Libraries Out of Use by 2020, http://news.bbc.co.uk/1/hi/uk/3661831.stm.

Johnson, A. and McSmith, A. (2006) Children Say Being Famous is Best Thing in World, *Independent*, 18 December, www.independent.co.uk/news/uk/this-britain/children-say-being-famous-is-best-thing-in-world-429000.html.

Keillor, G. (2007) *Speech at the Closing Session of the ALA Conference in Washington, DC, 26 June,* see RealPlayer RealVideo file at rtsp://video.c-span.org/archive/arc_btv/btv071407_4c.rm.

Usherwood, B. (2007) *Equity and Excellence in the Public Library: why ignorance is not our heritage*, Ashgate.

Selected reading

Public library history

Aitken, W. R. (1971) *A History of the Public Library Movement in Scotland to 1955*, Scottish Library Association.

Black, A. (1996) *A New History of the English Public Library: social and intellectual contexts, 1850–1914*, Leicester University Press.

Black, A. (2000) *The Public Library in Britain 1914–2000*, British Library.

Black, A. (2001) The Victorian Information Society: surveillance, bureaucracy, and public librarianship in 19th-century Britain, *Information Society*, **17** (1), 63–80.

Greenwood, T. G. (1891) *Public Libraries: a history of the movement and a manual for the organization and management of rate supported libraries*, Cassell & Company.

Hendry, J. D. (1974) *A Social History of Branch Library Development: with special reference to the City of Glasgow*, Scottish Library Association.

House of Commons (1849) *Report of the Select Committee on Public Libraries Together with the Minutes of Evidence and Appendix*, House of Commons.

Jackson, S. L. (1974) *Libraries and Librarianship in the West: a brief history*, McGraw-Hill.

Kelly, T. (1966) *Public Libraries in Great Britain before 1850*, Library Association.

Kelly, T. (1977) *History of Public Libraries in Great Britain 1845–1975*, Library Association.

Kelly, T. and Kelly, E. (1977) *Books for the People: an illustrated history of the British public library*, Andre Deutsch.

McColvin, L. (1942) *Public Library System of Great Britain*, Library Association.

McColvin, L. (1956) *The Chance to Read: public libraries in the world today*, Phoenix House.

Minto, J. (1932) *A History of the Public Library Movement in Great Britain and Ireland*, George Allen & Unwin and The Library Association.

Murison, W. J. (1971) *The Public Library: its origins, purpose, and significance*, 2nd edn, George G. Harrap.

Sturges, P. (1996) Conceptualizing the Public Library 1850–1919. In Kinnell, M. and Sturges, P. (eds), *Continuity and Innovation in the Public Library: the development of a social institution*, Library Association.

Sykes, P. (1979) *The Public Library in Perspective: an examination of its origins and modern role*, Clive Bingley.

Whiteman, P. (1986) *Public Libraries Since 1945: the impact of the McColvin Report*, Clive Bingley.

Issues in professional practice

Feather, J. (2008) *The Information Society: a study of continuity and change*, 5th edn, Facet Publishing.

Goulding, A. (2006) *Public Libraries in the 21st Century: defining services and debating the future*, Ashgate.

McCook, K. de la Pena (2004) *Introduction to Public Librarianship*, Neal-Schuman.

Train, B., Dalton, P. and Elkin, J. (2000) Embracing Inclusion: the critical role of the library, *Library Management*, **21** (9), 483–90.

Usherwood, B. (1989) *The Public Library as Public Knowledge*, Library Association Publishing.

Usherwood, B. (1993) *Public Library Politics: the role of the elected member*, Library Association Publishing.

Usherwood, B. (2007) *Equity and Excellence in the Public Library: why ignorance is not our heritage*, Ashgate.

Wilson, K. and Birdi, B. (2008) *The Right 'Man' for the Job? The role of empathy in community librarianship*, Department of Information Studies, University of Sheffield.

Major government and government-sponsored reports (1997–)

Culture, Media and Sport Committee (2005) *Public Libraries – Third Report of Session 2004-2005*, Culture, Media and Sport Committee, House of Commons.

DCMS (1999) *Libraries for All: social inclusion in public libraries*, Department for Culture, Media and Sport.

DCMS (2003) *Framework for the Future: libraries, learning and information in the next decade*, Department for Culture, Media and Sport.

Dolan, J. (2007) *Blueprint for Excellence – public libraries 2008-2011: 'Connecting people to knowledge and inspiration'*, Museums, Libraries and Archives Council.

Muddiman, D., Durrani, S., Dutch, M., Linley, R., Pateman, J. and Vincent, J. (2000) *Open to All? The public library and social exclusion*, Resource.

Resource and CABE (2003) *Better Public Libraries*, Resource and the Centre for Architecture and the Built Environment, www.mla.gov.uk/resources/assets//I/id874rep_pdf_6757.pdf.

Think tank reports

Adam Smith Institute (1986) *Ex Libris*, ASI (Research) Ltd.

Brandon, J. and Murray, D. (2007) *Hate on the State: how British libraries encourage Islamic extremism*, Centre for Social Cohesion, www.socialcohesion.co.uk/pdf/HateOnTheState.pdf.

Coates, T. (2004) *Who's in Charge? Responsibility for the public library service*, Libri Trust.

Leadbetter, C. (2003) *Overdue: how to create a modern public library service*, Demos, www.demos.co.uk/files/overdue.pdf.

Index

The Public Library Training Handbook
A frontline service delivery manual
David McMenemy and Christine Rooney-Browne

The staffing profiles of public libraries are currently undergoing much change, and the public interface is increasingly being staffed by non-professional personnel, in many cases with no professional librarians on site to offer advice and experience. This situation requires a well trained and knowledgeable workforce, able to operate in all the practical everyday areas where professional knowledge had previously been necessary to deliver a good frontline service.

It is also vital that frontline staff should have a clear understanding of the ethos of public library service provision, a topic widely covered for professional staff in library schools, together with knowledge of the local government context and the various initiatives proposed centrally and locally that impact on user expectation and service delivery.

It is of paramount importance that there should be made available accessible training materials addressing these issues for paraprofessional staff in public libraries, and this handbook fulfils that need. It covers all the challenges facing staff on a day-to-day basis in public libraries, including the following knowledge and skills:

- what is a public library?
- the central and local government context
- public library services
- handling reference enquiries
- understanding the legal obligations of the public library
- essential ICT skills
- reader development and book promotion
- working with children and young people
- understanding the performance measurement regime
- customer care and assertiveness
- developing skills for the future.

Downloadable training materials in the format of customizable PowerPoint slides will be available online, making the book easily usable for induction of new staff.

This handbook is essential reading for all public library paraprofessional staff and their managers and trainers. In the UK it will be of great assistance to any individuals wishing to undertake the ACLIP route through CILIP's Framework of Qualifications, but it also addresses global issues.

2009; 192pp; paperback; 978-1-85604-645-9; £44.95

The Academic Library
Second edition
Peter Brophy

Reviews of the previous edition
'*The Academic Library* should be on every student librarian's core reading list.'
INFORMATION WORLD REVIEW
'An excellent book . . .Peter Brophy has achieved a worthy and useful summary of the academic library at the start of the new millennium.'

SCONUL NEWSLETTER

This authoritative and wide-ranging textbook provides a comprehensive overview of the changing functions of higher education libraries and the organizational cultures in which they operate. It offers an assessment of the impact of such changes on service delivery from both provider and user perspectives, and considers the future role of the academic library.

The second edition has been completely updated, with a new chapter on performance measurement and more extensive coverage of: accessibility; information literacy; portals; digital libraries; copyright; institutional repositories; virtual and managed learning environments; and management of change. Written in a readable and accessible style, the book focuses on:
- the library in the institution
- users of the academic library
- the impacts and opportunities of ICTs
- human resources
- management and organization of resources
- collection and access management
- the academic library building
- library systems and networks
- specialist services
- management and professional issues
- the academic library of the future.

This textbook is an indispensable introduction to the range of issues facing academic libraries for students and new professionals. It also makes stimulating reading for education administrators and academic library managers in both higher and further education.

2005; 248pp; paperback; 1-85604-527-8; £34.95

Delivering the Best Start

A guide to early years libraries

Carolynn Rankin and Avril Brock

The Early Years Foundation Stage (EYFS) is now statutory in the UK for children from birth to five years, and other countries are experiencing similar developments; early years librarians, teachers, nursery nurses, playgroup leaders and childminders all require knowledge of how to promote and encourage communication, language and literary skills. Parental reading with young children is clearly vitally important, and libraries are uniquely placed to support the development of literacy skills in pre-school children.

This book provides an understanding of how children develop such skills through enjoyable and meaningful learning experiences, and is a pioneering practical guide for library and information professionals involved in planning and delivering services in early years libraries. Drawing on the authors' underpinning contemporary research and examples from current best practice, it will equip practitioners with a broad range of knowledge and ideas. Key areas covered include:

- take them to the library: the role of the early years professional
- people and partnerships: working across disciplinary boundaries, and how to involve parents and carers
- buildings, design and space: the children's libraries of the future
- resources for early years libraries: books, toys and other delights
- reaching your audience: the librarian's role
- planning and organizing: projects and reading sessions.

User-friendly and accessible, each chapter is clearly structured and sets out the key issues for practitioners, scenarios offering insights into these, and practical ideas and resources for service provision. The book also includes case studies of successful pre-school library initiatives in a variety of global settings, useful information about relevant organizations, and links to helpful websites.

This valuable text is essential reading for all library and information professionals working with young children – whether those with responsibility for the strategic planning of services, or those involved in delivering them at community level. Essential for students of library and information studies or childhood studies, and practitioners undertaking NVQ qualifications, it also provides a sound background in early years literacy and provision for a range of local authority practitioners, such as nursery teachers and children's centre managers.

2008; 208pp; paperback; 978-1-85604-610-7; £39.95

Better by Design

An introduction to planning and designing a new library building

Ayub Khan

Libraries today are faced with rapidly shifting populations of users with differing needs, who require a range of new communications links that are transforming our concept of the library space. This developing role has created a set of new and complex challenges for those delivering library services.

There is no such thing as the 'perfect' library building. However, a well designed building will enable a project both to gain local acceptance more easily and to ease the process of securing planning permission. It also needs to be cost effective to run, support the organization's objectives well, offer an improved service to the user and make an impact on the community.

This much needed book takes as its starting point the fact that few architects know very much about libraries, and fewer librarians know about architectural planning and design. It steers a clear path for library managers through the language and processes that they need to understand as members of a team overseeing the planning of a new library building project, major refurbishment or remodelling of an existing library. Key topics include:

- twenty-first century libraries
- developing a business case
- project management
- the design/project team
- selecting an architect
- partnership and community engagement
- the design brief
- design quality
- space planning and access
- occupancy and post-occupancy evaluation
- building libraries for the future.

Appendices offer top tips and checklists, together with a glossary of common terms used within the construction environment to help further de-mystify the design process for librarians. This practical and accessible book is an invaluable guide not only for new entrants to the library profession, but also for experienced practitioners who are approaching for the first time the important task of creating a new library or major refurbishment of existing facilities. It will also be of great relevance to architects unfamiliar with library building requirements.

2008; 224pp; hardback; 978-1-85604-650-3; £44.95